the **ULTIMATE SALES MANAGER** PLAYBOOK

Advance Praise for

the ULTIMATE SALES MANAGER PLAYBOOK

"Sales leadership advice is abundant and overflowing on websites, podcasts, books, and more. But sales wisdom, that is a rare and highly valued resource. You know that it's wisdom when it lasts the test of time, technology, and trends. Bill Zipp's *Ultimate Sales Manager Playbook* provides new and experienced sales leaders with a roadmap and practical wisdom at each stage of the process. This book is destined to be an instant classic and required reading for all who aspire to lead the way that Bill has done for his entire life."

—**Jim Gallic**, Regional Vice President, Welltok, Inc

"There are thousands of management books out there but few get into the reality of what it take to be a successful *sales* leader. This book takes years of invaluable experience and boils it down to actionable steps sales leaders at all levels can take to have a positive impact. Not sometime next year, but immediately."

—**Ben Brewer**, Chief Revenue Officer, Nintex

"Bill Zipp has always exhibited the knack for 'keeping it real' and truly getting to the point of what matters most—providing simple, practical, effective methods to help sales leaders and sellers succeed consistently. No fluff! The sales manager is the pivotal role in any sales organization, where the rubber meets the road and the strategy either turns into new revenue or it doesn't. In this playbook, Bill once again takes the complex reality of the sales manager role and transforms it to simple and easily applied 'big rocks.' Motivate! Mobilize! Multiply! Sales leaders simply cannot build a sustainable business or career by hitting the "more button." By learning and applying Bill's inside-out mindset in this playbook, sales managers will change their careers and their lives.

—**Chris Brantman**, Division Vice-President, ADP Major Accounts

"Bill's approach of people first creates sustainable success. I have benefited from Bill's ideas and coaching over the years and owe much of my success to him!"

—**Loren Brockhouse**, Chief Revenue Officer, Vanco

"The true leverage point in sales is sales management, and no-one understands how to optimize this role like Bill Zipp. *The Ultimate Sales Manager Playbook* is hands-on, practical, and road-tested. It sets out all the key strategies for helping your salespeople succeed and be the best they can be, including winning their trust, coaching them, rewarding them, setting appropriate goals, and much more. If you manage sellers--read this now."

—**Andrew Sobel**, President, Andrew Sobel Advisors, Inc., bestselling author of *It Starts with Clients, Power Questions* and *Clients for Life.*

"Bill is spot on in his approach to sales leadership. But more importantly, he's real and authentic. His heart comes out on every page, and, having worked with him over the past ten plus years, he's consistently consistent. What he writes are truly his beliefs and the behaviors he exhibits."

—**Candace Horton**, Leadership Development Consultant for Global Enablement SAP Concur

"The difference between a good salesperson and a great one is often dependent on the relationship a seller has with their manager. Sadly, too few salespeople have positive sales management experiences. The aim of this book is to change all that. Bill Zipp provides proven principles and practices for anyone who leads in the sales side of the business to deeply motivate and effectively mobilize their people to be the best at what they do."

—**Lisa Earle McLeod**, Founder, McLeod & More, Inc., bestselling author of *Selling with Noble Purpose*

"The leadership principles that I have learnt from Bill have given me the structure to help build, scale and develop high performing sales teams. His principles and practices have helped give me a structure that delivers success both at an individual contributor and leadership level."

—**Dafydd Llewellyn**, Regional Vice President,
UK and Emerging Markets Talend

"As a sales manager, you know what keeps you awake at night. Bill Zipp does, too, and in *The Ultimate Sales Manager Playbook*, he gives you concrete, actionable ideas and strategies to turn challenges into opportunities. Not a speck of theory in here because Bill has been there, done that, and knows what works in the real world of selling. Buy this book today!"

—**Joe Calloway**, bestselling author of *The Leadership Mindset*

"Bill's approach to sales leadership is practical, inspirational, and most importantly proven. This playbook gives sales leaders the tools they need to both motivate their people and ensure that their sales goals are met. This playbook will give you what you need to build a winning sales team!"

—**Crystal Wahle**, Senior Director Talent and Organization
Development Genesys

"Are you looking for a sales leadership book that will inspire you and your sales team to reach their highest level of potential? Bill Zipp, the expert, will guide you on that journey through an ever-changing sales environment. This book is a powerful 'how to' guide that provides a practical, uncomplicated, precise methodology for sales leaders at all levels. My recommendation is simple—read it, execute its recommendations, and share it with others who need it. It is that good."

—**Jeff Foley**, Brigadier General, U.S. Army (retired),
author of *BRAVE Business Leadership: Grow
Competent, Confident Leaders and Get Great Results.*

"Time is short, and attention spans are even shorter. To get our attention, authors write books entitled the seven habits of this and the three steps to that all in the hopes that we'll buy their book. And yes, people do buy their books, but in reality, people don't apply what they've read because it's not specific enough to act on, and it's not compelling enough to want to act on it. Bill Zipp's writing on sales, leadership, and strategy is the opposite. He's been essential reading of mine for over ten years, and everything I read of his (yes, everything) encourages me, excites me, and helps me grow as a leader and as a person. If you want to fast track your sales results, then read Bill Zipp. He's the real deal in sales and leadership."

—**Hugh Blane**, President, Claris Consulting, author of *Seven Principles of Transformational Leadership*

"After a thirty-four-year career at Eli Lilly and Company working in finance and manufacturing, I decided to set up my own consulting business. I knew nothing about 'sales.' Where do I start? Enter Bill Zipp as my sales coach. Bill immediately connected with me and gave me confidence in my ability to move forward. Our coaching sessions were fun and focused, and I even had 'a shoulder to cry on.' I always looked forward to the sessions from which I emerged fully motivated and energized. Bottom line, my business is currently two times of what I anticipated and has grown every year since I started five years ago."

—**Brendan Crowley**, Brendan Crowley Advisors, LLC

the
ULTIMATE
SALES
MANAGER
PLAYBOOK

Becoming a Successful Sales Leader

BILL ZIPP

NEW YORK

LONDON • NASHVILLE • MELBOURNE • VANCOUVER

the ULTIMATE SALES MANAGER PLAYBOOK
Becoming a Successful Sales Leader

© 2021 **BILL ZIPP**

Published in New York, New York, by Morgan James Publishing. Morgan James is a trademark of Morgan James, LLC. www.MorganJamesPublishing.com

ISBN 978-1-63195-083-4 paperback
ISBN 978-1-63195-084-1 eBook
Library of Congress Control Number: 2020904131

Cover Design by:
Rachel Lopez
www.r2cdesign.com

Morgan James is a proud partner of Habitat for Humanity Peninsula and Greater Williamsburg. Partners in building since 2006.

Get involved today! Visit
www.MorganJamesBuilds.com

To the many sales leaders at SAP Concur who enthusiastically embraced the earliest versions of these resources, thank you for trusting me!

TABLE OF CONTENTS

ACKNOWLEDGMENTS

There are so many people I need to thank for making the enormous privilege of working with sales leaders around the world—and by extension this book—even possible.

Cindy Domanowski, you were the first to trust me to work with your team. I owe you an enormous debt of gratitude. Mike D'Onofrio, thank you for your unbridled enthusiasm for my approach to sales leadership and always inviting me in to be with your people. Daffydd Llewellyn, you are the ultimate gentleman. Thank you for the opportunity to work with your team in the UK year after year. And I can't say enough about my SAP Concur colleagues, Christal Bemont, Crystal Wahle, Ben Brewer, and Bill Tillman. Thank you for letting me forge the early framework of this book with you.

A big thank you to Jeffrey Davis with Tracking Wonder, whose partnership at the beginning of this project pushed me to think creatively and write clearly. Thank you to Dave Sauer at Morgan James for

xiv | the **ULTIMATE SALES MANAGER** PLAYBOOK

immediately seeing value in this manuscript and to Cortney Donelson for turning my tangled English into readable prose.

My biggest thanks, however, goes to my wife Denise. Thank you for believing in me so many years ago when I walked away from a secure job and a regular paycheck to follow a crazy dream. Thank you for your patience in the slow seasons and your forgiveness of my many mistakes (how many websites have I had?). What's good in these pages is because of you. Finally, as a person of faith, I praise my God and Father for his amazing grace to me.

FOREWORD

Salespeople are the heroes of the commercial economy.

They're the ones on the frontlines of business, making contact with prospects and building a compelling case for engaging in a first conversation. They're the ones maintaining that engagement—against all odds and against all competitors—driving deals through the sales pipeline. They're the ones who close those deals and generate the critical lifeblood all businesses need: topline revenue.

But even heroes, like elite athletes from gymnastics to golf, need a coach. They need someone who believes in them and helps them be at the top of their game, the very best version of their sales self.

That's where the rub comes. Few salespeople have the privilege of having such a positive, productive relationship with their sales manager. For many, that relationship is adversarial, a necessary evil they must endure, like so many other obstacles they must endure to succeed in the world of sales.

Bill Zipp aims to change all that with *The Ultimate Sales Manager Playbook*. In this powerful book he gives you the secrets to becoming a successful sales leader.

Bill summarizes his approach in three words: motivate, mobilize, and multiply. It's a proven model for leading from the inside out.

Beginning with trust, the oxygen that allows all relationships to thrive, he shows you how to establish credibility with your team and how to create a winning sales culture that attracts the brightest and best to work for you. With these keys in place, you'll learn a model for coaching that equips you to come alongside your salespeople, from the newest recruit to the most seasoned seller, and provide the leadership they need when they need it.

Other vital sales management practices are presented here as well, like how to conduct an effective one-on-one (no one really tells you how to do this), how to lead productive team meetings, how to hire the very best salespeople, and how to keep both yourself and your sellers from derailing in their roles.

What's especially unique about this book is that it's not just a book; it's a playbook. Every chapter ends with a practical exercise that will help you grow your people and hit your number.

Finally, if you're a salesperson considering a move to sales management, there's a chapter specifically written for you. Too many sellers have blindly accepted a promotion like this and found the step up actually become a step down. Not because they're bad people, but because sales management isn't in their DNA.

So open the pages, start reading, and become the leader you were always meant to be.

—**Jeb Blount**, CEO Sales Gravy, Bestselling author of
Fanatical Prospecting, Sales EQ, Objections, and *Inked*

INTRODUCTION

You are the most important person in your sales organization. If you're responsible for the direct management of salespeople in your company, your ability to do that well is the difference between the success and failure of those salespeople, and ultimately, the success and failure the company.

It's just as simple as that.

You build pipeline and assure quota completion. You direct customer engagement and drive the engagement of your salespeople. You attract new recruits to join your team, top talent walking in the front door, and make sure no one walks out the back door either. You're held accountable for hitting a number yourself, while holding the sellers who work for you accountable for hitting their numbers as well.

You are a coach, a counselor, a champion, a confidant, and at times, even, a shoulder to cry on. You are a frontline sales manager, the most important person in your sales organization.

Other people get the glory for what you do. Your boss reports revenue generation to the C-Suite and receives congratulations there, accidentally forgetting to mention you in the conversation. That's okay. Playing those political games is not what you really want. Your salespeople get applause for their above goal performance. That's okay too. You really don't want another plaque to put on the wall or week-long trip away from your family you'll have to pay income tax on.

What do you want?

You want to learn how to do your job better. Not a little better, a lot better. You want real-world solutions to the very real-world problems you face every day. You want proven principles and practical steps of action you can take tomorrow morning to get the most out of your salespeople. And you want less sleepless nights (okay, a lot less sleepless nights), knowing that your leadership is the very best it can possibly be.

That's what this playbook is all about. From motivation—connecting with your salespeople in a way that lights a fire in their souls—to mobilization, coaching your salespeople to execute your sales process at the highest levels of excellence, it's all here. You'll learn how to establish trust, provide praise, build a winning sales culture, conduct effective one-on-one's, and make your meetings matter again, or perhaps, matter for the very first time. Then you'll learn how to take all that and multiply it in others through hiring well and promoting wisely.

The information in this book has been forged in the fires of decades of sales leadership. There's no snake oil or useless fluff. Everything here I've done myself, repeatedly. Everything here, I've taught other sales leaders like you to do, also repeatedly. As a result, our careers have been changed forever. It's time for you to experience that change as well.

Yes, you are a frontline sales manager, and this is your playbook. Get ready for the game of your life!

Chapter One

AMY, AUSTIN, AND ME

Amy's Story

The "more" button isn't working.

She's pressed it plenty of times, too. More calls, more meetings, more forecast, more accountability. None of these, however, have resulted in more sales.

That's what's gnawing at Amy as she begins another crazy-busy week as the sales manager at her fast-growing technology firm. She's got two reps above plan, two reps way below plan, two reps on the bubble, and two open seats.

Being a salesperson was so much easier. All she had to do was think about her own number, something she could control. Being responsible for eight salespeople and eight sales numbers, well ... that's a different story.

But being a sales rep has no future. At least not the future Amy dreams about. Ultimately, she wants to be a VP, maybe even a CEO somewhere, and a path to the C-Suite is through sales management. Successful sales management, that is.

But a dream like that seems ludicrous right now. Every time her sales approach goal, something bad happens. Last month, one of her best reps moved on to another company, and now she has to hit her quota with two fewer people (which means more work for her, a different kind of more button).

Last week a "guaranteed" big deal fell apart in close, and the customer signed with a competitor. The rep convinced her it was a sure thing, and she believed him. Now it's a total loss. "Do I have to go on every sales call myself to make sure we close business?" Amy wonders.

"Spend most of your time with your A-Players," the consultant said at the sales management seminar at the beginning of the year. So she did that, and things got worse. First, Amy's A-Players didn't want to spend time with her. Not that they were rude or anything. They just wanted to do things on their own without interference from a manager. Frankly, that's what Amy had preferred when she was selling. That's why they're A-Players.

While she was figuring this out, her bottom two reps continued to struggle. Now, no amount of help, it seems, will bring them back from the brink of another bad year. And that means a bad year for her, too. No bonus. No President's Club. No promotion. Again.

"Just fire them," Amy's manager had told her. "That'll wake everyone up!"

Then she'll have four open sales seats with no hope of filling them any time soon. Bad breath is better than no breath, right? But she wonders to herself, "If I don't fire them, maybe I'll be the one getting fired. Not good."

In her heart, however, Amy's not sure any of her reps should get fired, because she's not been able to give them the help they really need. Everyone in her world runs from one fire to another, from one crisis to another, with no real plan for penetrating the marketplace and no real path to hitting their numbers, other than the repeated command to, "Sell, sell, sell!"

The really weird thing about all this is that Amy loves sales. She loves the thrill of the hunt and the joy of building business. She loves being rewarded for her hard work and out-of-the-box thinking. She even loves sales management, when she has the time to really do it. But she doesn't love the grind of every day's unrealistic demands—constant email, endless meetings—and the powerlessness she feels trying to motivate salespeople who don't seem interested in being motivated by her (or anyone else, for that matter).

Austin's Story

Austin's "more" button is broken too.

On the surface, it looks like he's living the dream. As CEO of the company he started, which grosses $40 million in sales a year, it does look like a dream. The last few years, however, have been more of a nightmare.

Austin is the only person in his company who can sell anything. He's hired and fired more salespeople than he can count, and the group he has right now isn't any better. Almost all of the revenue his company brings in is dependent on him.

"Just sell!" he tells them repeatedly, but they just don't. So Austin is stuck, trapped in a business he can't get away from because it's critically dependent on him to generate revenue. No rest. No vacation. No fun.

And the worst part is this: Austin's company can do so much more than it's doing right now, perhaps even break the $100 million mark. He yearns to work on big-picture strategy—the view from 30,000 feet—but he keeps getting pulled back to ground zero, digging in the details of another deal that's just about to collapse in close.

"Work on your business, not in it," the consulting guru had advised him. But how do you do that when working on your business could result in the very loss of your business? "That's probably why the guy's a consultant and not a business owner," Austin mumbles to himself.

Last summer, he tried to take a month away from work to go on a road trip with his family to Washington, D.C. His wife planned out the entire itinerary with excursions to historical landmarks they both wanted the kids to see. But every day was interrupted with frantic texts and emergency emails, and by the end of the second week, Austin flew home to rescue a canceled contract that could have bankrupt the company.

He rescued it but lost precious time with his family.

Like Amy, Austin loves his business. It's his baby, after all. And he loves closing deals, but he doesn't love the fact that everything in it—especially sales—is dependent on him, and he feels painted into a corner. Trapped, really, in a prison of his own making. And he worries about the future. Who will buy this thing when they find out it's really just him and a bunch of good, but hopelessly passive, people?

Sales Force Frustration

These stories are not made up. They're a couple of the all too painful experiences of real people I've worked with who are struggling to succeed in sales leadership. The source of their frustration is what I call The Outside-In Fallacy, or simply, the "more" button.

The Outside-In Fallacy is an approach to managing salespeople that emphasizes external pressure to get them to comply with sales directives and meet their sales goals. When they don't, an outside-in manager presses even harder, demanding more calls, more meetings, more reports, and more use of sales force automation but to no avail. The "more" button doesn't work because that's not how people—especially salespeople—are wired.

Successful sales leadership, the kind of leadership that actually gets more sales, is dramatically different. It rejects The Outside-In Fallacy, sales management by force, and leads from the inside out. It lights a spark in a salesperson's soul, fans the flame of that fire, and then watches it burn, baby, burn.

Sales leadership from the inside out follows these three essentials, each flowing from one to the other:

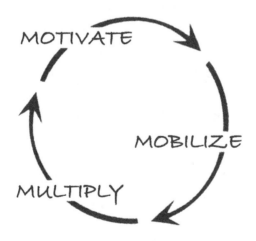

- **Motivate**: Connecting deeply as a sales leader with the salespeople who work for you so they trust you completely and let you unleash the power of their unique passion.
- **Mobilize**: Coaching the salespeople who work for you in the specific skills they need to execute the steps in your sales process at the highest levels of excellence.

- **Multiply**: Duplicating success in others by hiring and promoting the very best salespeople and sales managers, while keeping them from derailing in their roles.

The principles and practices of these essentials is the subject of this book. Additionally, we'll explore how to implement all three in the many meetings you attend as a sales leader, from one-on-one check-in's to team training. "Motivate, Mobilize, and Multiply" has the potential to transform your salespeople into a powerful force in the marketplace, because that's what it did for me.

My Story

Amy and Austin's story is my story too. I was good at selling and loved it. I was the fastest account executive in my company to reach $250,000 in sales, and then the fastest to a million dollars in sales. I won contests, made lots of money, and had a ton of fun.

Then it happened. I became a sales manager, and my real education began.

First, I learned that the salespeople who worked for me were not me. (Imagine that!) They weren't motivated by the things that motivated me. They didn't prospect the way I prospected, they didn't conduct sales calls the way I conducted sales calls, and they didn't close business the way I closed business. In other words, I couldn't hit our numbers by cloning myself. I had to learn how to lead.

Second, I discovered the team didn't trust me either. My aggressive style, which had worked so well in the marketplace, alienated the rest of the team. They could ignore it when I was their colleague, but they couldn't when I became their manager. I had some major bridge building to do.

And finally, I learned that I didn't know the first thing about coaching, the all-important skill for developing successful sales representatives. I talked too much and rarely listened. I hijacked calls and pressed my own agenda. I tried to be a sales superstar, ready and willing to close any deal at any time and stunted the growth of every member of my team. I was my own worst enemy, until I found a better way.

That better way is the subject of this book.

Why Read This Book?

Okay, okay, I can almost hear what you're thinking. *There are thousands of books out there on sales and leadership, so why should I read this one?* Am I right?

I also know that as a sales leader, you've endured a barrage of useless training initiatives, which had nothing to do with how things actually work in the real world, and you vowed not to waste another minute of your life with any book, video, podcast, or workshop that takes you away from your job—making more money.

I know these things because, like you, I've lived them. I've wasted my hard-earned money on plenty of bad books and sat through my share of useless training. So, here's my promise to you. Everything in this book—everything—has been forged in the fire of the real world of sales. There's no filler, no fluff, no fake news.

Here's what you'll find in its pages, and, perhaps, nowhere else:

- How the sales persona is different than any other kind of workplace persona and why motivating sellers from the inside out is critically important for success.
- Why building a great sales culture, the internal operating system of your organization, needs to become one of your top leadership priorities and how to do it.
- What the difference is between performance goals and process goals and why defining both clearly are key to hitting your number.

- How sales coaching is much more than cheerleading, what most coaching today has become, and how to master its specific skills.
- How to transform your one-on-one meetings and sales team meetings from the useless waste of time they are right now into powerful performance producers.
- How hiring salespeople is different than hiring anyone else in the world—all sales hires present well—and how to inject truth serum into the hiring process so the brightest and the best end up working for you.
- How to protect your personal and professional effectiveness from the leadership derailers that will destroy your career.

Here's How to Use This Book

So, I've convinced you to read this far. Stay with me, please. Okay? Here's how to use this book to your greatest advantage. Each section has a sequence to it, and there is a sequence within each sequence. In other words, mobilizing your sales force works best when you know how to motivate them first. Multiplying your sales force can only happen when you've mastered motivation and mobilization.

Additionally, each section has its own sequence. As you'll read soon enough—contrary to popular opinion—successful sales leaders don't start with *why*, they start with *who*. Your salespeople will not trust your attempts to tap their inner motivators until they trust you. *Who* comes first, then *why*. Once they trust you, however, they'll let you light the fire of their unique *why*, and you'll get to pour gas on the flame with gallons of positive praise. That's the sequence of **Section One: Motivate.**

Section Two: Mobilize also has a step-by-step sequence to it. Sales mobilization begins with goal clarity. Without specifically defined performance goals and specifically defined process goals—not one or the other, but both—you have nothing to mobilize your team to achieve. Clarity is not enough, however. All of us need someone outside of ourselves helping us reach our goals. Salespeople thrive when their manager knows how to come alongside and coach them to greatness.

Here is where I depart from popular opinion about coaching, however. Coaching gurus will tell you to detach yourself from outcomes when you coach others. Being attached to outcomes, they say, causes you to press too hard and keeps people from actually achieving them. Nothing could be further from the truth! Sales coaching begins with outcomes because that is where the sales profession begins—outcomes—and where it will end if you don't produce them.

I'll show you how to implement just the opposite: outcome-based sales coaching. Not as a tool, however, to beat up your salespeople (or keep them from being good Buddhists, who live a life detached from outcomes). Outcome-based sales coaching doesn't pretend that results don't matter in business and is fully aware of the revenue it's accountable for generating. But neither is it afraid of those outcomes. It embraces them fully with faith and courage, helping salespeople become the very best version of themselves in the actual process of achieving them.

Finally, motivation and mobilization provide a template to re-think all your many meetings, so they become powerful tools in your toolkit and not the useless waste of time they are right now. And motivation and mobilization are what you multiply in others as you bring new salespeople onto your team and promote successful individual contributors into leadership roles. So, start at the beginning of this book and work your way through each sequence, and the sequence within each sequence, seeking to master the principles and practices in the order in which they're given.

There are two exceptions to this sequencing. If you, or a salesperson you know, is being considered for a promotion from individual contributor to sales manager, read Chapter Eleven immediately and complete the questionnaire at the end of the chapter. You'll thank me later. And if you're on the edge of burn-out and your role as a sales leader is driving you crazy, jump to Chapter Twelve and get back in control of your life. Then read each of the sections and process the sequencing in turn.

Real Work Alert

A unique feature of this book is that in every chapter, I've provided an opportunity for you to practically apply the topic being discussed. This makes what you have in your hands not just a book but a playbook. Like driving a car, successful sales leadership is a skill that's learned by actually driving a car, not discussing the theories of automotive transportation. If you take the time to complete each activity, your understanding of sales leadership will make that all-important leap from mere theory to practice.

These application exercises are highlighted by the words "Real Work Alert." As with the content that accompanies them, each exercise has been forged in the fire of the real world of sales. No fluff! In addition to being embedded in each chapter, I've put them all together in the back of the book under Sales Leadership Resources, and they're also available online at www.billzipp.com/salessuccess.

Amy, Austin, and You

Little by little, I learned how to motivate and mobilize the members of my sales team. I was able to use my new-found leadership skills, both one-on-one and in a group, to grow each member of our team, and soon the brightest and best in our industry came to work for us. In a few years, we nearly doubled our direct sales revenue and won national recognition for our contribution to the field of nontraditional revenue development. Alas, another piece of education awaited me when I became CEO of the company, but that's another story.

Austin found a way out of his self-imposed prison as well. It began by identifying the specific steps of action needed to execute his sales process. These were things he was doing intuitively, almost unconsciously, but didn't ever define them. A team of salespeople was assembled whose mission it was to execute these steps consistently, and resources were given to this team to master them completely. Soon his company grew by 50% and is today knocking on the door of $100 million of annual revenue. More importantly, sales income is equally distributed among the entire team, and Austin is able to go on vacation with his family.

And Amy?

Amy, too, learned how to motivate and mobilize the salespeople who worked for her. The leadership she brought to her team turned around not only a bad year but her entire career. She never looked back and gained a stellar reputation as a sales leader everyone wanted to work for. She now sits in the C-Suite of her very own start-up technology company.

Now it's your turn to motivate, mobilize, and multiply your sales force. Turn the page, it's going to be a wide ride!

PART I

MOTIVATION

"The authentic way to increase shareholder value is with a purpose that inspires employees to create innovative products and provide superior service to customers. When employees believe their work has a deeper meaning, their results will vastly exceed those who only use their minds and their bodies."[1]

—Bill George

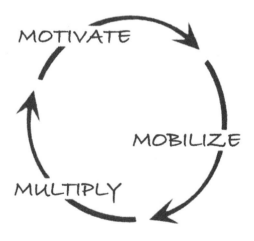

Chapter Two

TRUST

I'm standing atop a tall building. We walk past the "Danger" and "No Public Access" signs—written in red with big, bold letters—ignoring them like playground children. My feet feel the hard edge of the rooftop line. Below, open air.

"Trust me, jump," are the words I hear whispered in my ear. "Trust me."

And then I wake up.

It's a recurring dream of mine. Sometimes, I'm on the top of a building, sometimes on the edge of a bridge, and sometimes, on the side of a cliff.

The meaning of this dream, I'm sure, lies buried in some obscure childhood experience. (The flying monkeys in *The Wizard of Oz*, perhaps? They really creeped me out.) I never jump. I always wake up with "trust me" echoing inside my head.

From the perspective of your sales reps, this is exactly what you're doing as a leader. When you ask them to call on a new prospect, when you ask them to pitch a new product, when you ask them to use a new relationship management system upon which their entire livelihood depends, you're saying, "Jump … Jump now!" And when they hesitate, you whisper (or perhaps shout), "Trust me. I'm your manager."

Which, oddly enough, doesn't convince them to jump. They trusted a manager once, and it didn't end well. S–P–L–A–T.

So you're stuck, and so are they, frozen on a ledge, taking no action at all.

Start with Who, Not with Why

Much has been written recently on creating a motivational environment in the workplace. Shocking employee disengagement statistics have driven us to seriously consider this dynamic. It doesn't take a genius to figure out that if a person doesn't care about his or her work, the work will suffer (and the business with it). As an antidote to disengagement, we've been told as leaders to start with why, because why provides the real reasons human beings need to do their very best work.

This is true. I devote the entire next chapter on how to create a motivational environment in the sales context. But in my experience, you can't start with why, you must start with who. Let me explain…

While human beings aren't robots and need real reasons to get things done, these same human beings are wary of being manipulated by these reasons. Again, unlike robots, you can't put a gigabyte of motivation in to get a gigabyte of motivation out. It doesn't work that way, especially when those human beings have been around the block a bit and burned more than once by misdirected motivational initiatives.

In other words, your salespeople refuse to jump because they don't trust you. Nothing personal, that's just the way it is. And all the platitudes in the world—even profound poetic platitudes on posters with panoramic views—won't convince them.

Why? Because you can't motivate someone who doesn't trust you. It just won't work. Any attempts will be seen as crass manipulation or not motivation at all.

So, we begin with trust. And that means we begin with you. A you, that is, who is worthy of your salespeople's trust. How do you become that kind of leader? Three things are crucial: character, competence, and chemistry. Or what I call the Trust Triad.

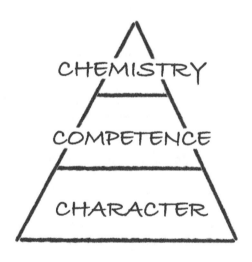

Trust Triad One: Character

At the bottom of the Trust Triad is character. It's at the base, foundational in force, for a reason. It's here where trust begins. If you, as a leader, aren't a credible person with a reliable character, nothing else matters.

Character means that you're a man or woman of your word: you do what you say you'll do. It means your salespeople can depend on you, and you'd never ask them to do something you wouldn't do yourself (like jumping off a building, a bridge, or a cliff). And character means you act this way when things are going well and when things are going poorly, when you're having a good day and when you're having a bad one.

Hall of Fame basketball coach John Wooden once wrote, "The true test of a man's character is what he does when no one's watching." Wise words from the Wizard of Westwood. That's the point, isn't it? Character's not dependent on the public eye to perform. It acts consistent with its values, even in private.

While entire volumes have been written on character, here are five fundamental questions to ask yourself to check your character as a leader:

- Do you practice what you preach? Are the actions you take as a leader fully aligned with the words you say?
- Do you honor your word? When you say you're going to do something, do you do it *without exception*?
- Are you genuine and real? Have you dropped the chest-thumping bravado and ego-driven head games, which so many leaders play?
- Do you say you're sorry when you're wrong? When you make a mistake, do you admit it, openly and honestly, and move on?
- Are you a living, breathing example of the values your company is committed to? Are you asking people to do things that you're not doing yourself on a consistent basis?

Character is the starting point for successful sales leadership. Remove the foundation from under a house, and the building collapses. Remove the engine from a car, and it cannot be driven down the road. Remove oxygen from the air, and people stop breathing. Pick your metaphor, and you'll be spot on about character. Remove it from leadership, and all is lost.

"We trust—and follow—people who are real, who are consistent, whose behavior, values, and beliefs are aligned," wrote Richard Boyatzis and Annie McKee in *Resonant Leadership*. "We trust people whom we do not constantly have to second-guess."[2]

Be this kind of leader.

Trust Triad Two: Competence

But character isn't enough. We've all worked with someone about whom we could say, "He's a heck of a guy but just doesn't get stuff done." Is that person you? Don't let it be. In addition to unquestionable character, become a sales leader of unparalleled competence, a sales leader who gets stuff done. Done well. Done completely. Done on time.

Competence has to do with your professional responsibilities and how fully you execute them. It's born from a commitment to master the demands of your job, not for ego or self-glorification, but to maximize your influence with others. It's the platform, so to speak, you stand on to be heard by your salespeople. Being good at what you do leads to increased followership every time.

If you're choosing a doctor to perform open heart surgery, you want someone who won't advise a drastic procedure like this unless it is absolutely necessary and won't add expensive extras to pad profit. But you also want a doctor who won't accidentally nick an artery and leave you dying on the operating table. In other words, you want a surgeon you can trust, both in their personal character and their professional competence.

People want both in their leaders as well. Here are five questions to ask yourself to check your competence as a leader:

- Do you have a clear grasp of the key responsibilities of your position and fulfill those responsibilities at the highest levels of excellence?

- Do you have a reliable system that captures your activities and appointments, so no detail or deadline gets missed?

- Do you process your email in a prompt and productive manner, getting back to team members who contact you during the workweek within twenty-four hours?

- Do you facilitate the meetings you run—your most public leadership activity—in a businesslike manner, starting on time, ending on time, and staying on track with the top priorities of the agenda?

- Is your physical appearance and dress sharp and professional, always appropriate for the various business situations you find yourself in?

Trust Triad Three: Chemistry

The final piece of the Trust Triad is chemistry. A squishy word, to be sure, compared to character and competence. But don't be fooled by its squishiness, it isn't easy to pull off.

What I mean by chemistry is the ability of a leader to connect with people and spark a meaningful relationship. A warm smile, a firm handshake, eye contact, and a genuine compliment all combine to forge a powerful chemical compound: humanity.

A leader who stands aloof, a leader who laughs at others but never at himself, a leader who's always busy, bothered, and burdened, won't be leading for very long. Return to our surgeon analogy. You want a medical professional with character and competence, yes, but you also want someone who cares for you as a patient and communicates that care in a compassionate way. This is commonly referred to as having a good "bedside manner," and if you've ever had a doctor without one, you know how painful it can be. So it is with leadership.

"But I'm not a people person!" you counter. That's fine to say if you're an individual contributor working in an isolated cubicle (maybe). But the minute you took on the role of sales manager, you took on the mantle of leadership, and that mantle comes with the mandate to connect with people. It's not optional now.

This doesn't mean you must become a backslapping politician, the rare breed of person who never met a stranger and never forgets a name. Most of us are not that person (thank God). Each of us connects with others in our own unique way. The important thing is to be true to our self, comfortable in our own skin. Authenticity like that causes people to trust us, often in an instant.

There are two distinct domains in which chemistry occurs, and each one has different dynamics. There's the one-on-one domain and the group domain. Both must be mastered for sales leadership success.

One-on-One Chemistry

As an extrovert, I'm much more comfortable in a group setting than in an individual one. Give me an audience, and I'm like a fish in water (a pig in mud?). As a result of this personality trait, having exceptional one-on-one meetings was not something that came naturally to me. My first attempts were painfully awkward, but I knew it was a skill I had to learn to be an effective leader. When I finally did learn it, I was shocked at the power it had to connect deeply with people.

Here's the honest truth about one-on-one interaction: People may forget what you have to say in a public presentation, but they will never forget how you made them feel in a private, personal encounter. Good *or* bad. This kind of chemistry is essential for successful sales leadership, and like I said, it can be learned. Even enjoyed!

Here are five questions to ask yourself to check your one-on-one chemistry as a leader:

- Are you fully present in the one-on-one meetings you attend? Have you eliminated all distractions (and potential distractions), like a ringing phone or pinging notifications?
- Do you actively listen to the people you're with in a one-on-one meeting? Are you paying attention to what they're really saying, not just their words but the emotions behind them?
- Does your physical posture reflect your personal presence? Do you lean forward, make eye contact, and nod your head, fully engaged in the conversation?
- Do you ask good questions? Do you help people clarify their thoughts by posing open-ended questions that allow them to explore the issues at hand more deeply?
- Do you make a point to find something you can honestly affirm, compliment, or praise in the course of your conversations?

Group Chemistry

I once received a piece of painful, but extraordinarily helpful, feedback from an attendee at a workshop I was leading. In the comment section at the bottom of the evaluation form, the person wrote, "When I came into the room, the presenter looked mad and angry. I almost walked out, but I'm glad I stayed because the content was really good."

Ouch!

I remember that workshop well. The conference presenter before me went late, and I was frantically trying to get my laptop to sync with the projector. Nothing was working, and as people filed in, I wasn't ready to start and had to skip a critical final review of my notes. It was super stressful, and the stress had gotten to me.

I also know that I'm afflicted with a syndrome referred to as Resting Angry Face (known in less polite circles by another term. Google it.). Resting Angry Face is a facial expression that unintentionally appears as if you're annoyed, irritated, or contemptuous. Which is *not* how I feel about people. But before the start of this workshop, the opposite appeared to be true.

In sales leadership, you'll find yourself in similar situations, perhaps with similar facial challenges. Here are five questions to ask yourself to check your group chemistry as a leader:

- Are you fully prepared for your group meetings, so your mind and emotions are calm and confident? This includes all preparations related to physical arrangements and technology.
- Do you schedule extra time before and/or after your group meetings to make important informal connections with the people in attendance?
- Have you thought through ways to make your group meetings fully interactive, so you aren't the only one talking in them?
- Do you have a strategy to help you stop, take a deep breath, make eye contact, and smile at the beginning, middle, and end of your group meetings?
- Do you make a point to authentically thank, recognize, or praise someone in attendance and/or the entire group at your group meetings?

Who, Why, and How to Work with Millennials

I hope I've convinced you to start with who, not why. Why is important, and it's the subject of the next chapter. But why sits on the foundation of who, or else it will be rejected as another attempt by management to manipulate the masses.

This brings me to millennials, that wonderfully gifted and immensely talented generation born between 1982 and 2004, entering the workforce by the thousands. This group of young adults was raised in an era where they expected to be lied to by the media, by businesses, and by their government. Previous generations gave a presumption of innocence to these social institutions. Not millennials. Millennials' default position is this: I'm being lied to, and you've got to prove it to me otherwise.

And who can blame them? Look at the long string of scandals they've seen in their short lifetimes. It's enough to sour the most optimistic soul. Which is another reason to start with who and not why. In working with millennials, pay extremely close attention to your character, your competence, and your chemistry, or they won't believe a single thing you say, no matter how motivational it appears to be. The payoff will be a loyalty from them that you never dreamed possible.

Real Work Alert

Here's your first real work assignment. All twenty of the Trust Triad questions above are in a self-scoring survey immediately below. Complete this survey by rating yourself on each item, from 1 (almost never) to 5 (almost always). Add your scores at the bottom of the questionnaire for a percentage rating, then answer the three follow-up questions after the survey.

TRUST TRIAD QUESTION	Almost Never / Almost Always				
1. Do you practice what you preach? Are the actions you take as a leader fully aligned with words you say?	1	2	3	4	5
2. Do you honor your word? When you say you're going to do something, do you do it *without exception*?	1	2	3	4	5

3.	Are you genuine and real? Have you dropped the chest-thumping bravado and ego-driven games that so many sales leaders play?	1	2	3	4	5
4.	Do you say sorry when you're wrong? When you make a mistake, do you admit it—openly and honestly—and move on?	1	2	3	4	5
5.	Are you a living example of the mission and values of your company? Are you asking people to do things that you're not doing yourself on a consistent basis?	1	2	3	4	5
6.	Do you have a clear grasp of the key responsibilities of your position and fulfill those responsibilities at the highest levels of excellence?	1	2	3	4	5
7.	Do you have a reliable system that captures your activities and appointments, so no detail or deadline gets dropped?	1	2	3	4	5
8.	Do you process your email in a prompt and productive manner, getting back to team members who contact you during the work week within 24 hours?	1	2	3	4	5

9. Do you facilitate the meetings you run in a businesslike manner, starting on time, ending on time, and staying on track with the items on the agenda?	1	2	3	4	5
10. Is your physical appearance and dress sharp and professional, always appropriate for the various business situations in which you find yourself?	1	2	3	4	5
11. Are you fully present in the meetings you attend? Have you eliminated all distractions (and potential distractions), like a ringing phone or pinging notifications?	1	2	3	4	5
12. Do you actively listen to the people you're with in a meeting? Do you pay attention to what they're really saying, not just their words but the emotions behind them?	1	2	3	4	5
13. Does your physical posture reflect your personal presence? Do you lean forward, make eye contact, nod your head, fully engaged in the conversation?	1	2	3	4	5

14. Do you ask good questions? Do you help people clarify their thoughts by posing open-ended queries that allow them to explore the issues at hand more deeply?	1	2	3	4	5
15. Do you make a point to find something you can honestly affirm, compliment, or praise in the course of your conversations?	1	2	3	4	5
16. Are you fully prepared for your team meetings, so your mind and emotions are confident and calm? This includes preparations related to physical arrangements and technology.	1	2	3	4	5
17. Do you schedule extra time before and/or after your team meetings to make informal connections with the people in attendance?	1	2	3	4	5
18. Have you thought through ways to make your team meetings fully interactive, so you aren't the only one talking in them?	1	2	3	4	5

19. Do you have a way to remind yourself to stop, take a deep breath, make eye contact, and smile at the beginning, middle, and end of your team meetings?	1	2	3	4	5
20. Do you make a point to authentically thank, recognize, or praise someone in attendance and/ or the entire group at your team meetings?	1	2	3	4	5
TOTAL					out of 100

A digital version of this survey is available online at www.billzipp.com/salessuccess.

What *Trust Triad* questions did you score the highest in? What is it about your leadership that causes you to excel in these areas?

What *Trust Triad* questions did you score the lowest in? What does this reveal about areas of your leadership that need to be strengthened?

What's one specific step of action you can take to improve in a *Trust Triad* area?

Consider having someone in your life whom you trust to complete this survey on you and discuss with you their perspective on your leadership.

Chapter Three
PASSION

I n Greek mythology, Sisyphus was the god of commerce and travel. He was not a good god, however, which provided an explanation to the ancient Greeks—wrong as it was—for business deals gone bad and tragedies at sea. Zeus looked the other way as Sisyphus carried out his crimes against humanity, but one day he crossed the line. On that day, Sisyphus committed an act so heinous that Zeus had to punish him.

For the rest of eternity, Sisyphus was condemned to push a big rock up a tall mountain. Just as he reached the top of the mountain, the rock would roll to the bottom, and Sisyphus would have to start all over again.

All day, every day.

Here the ancient Greeks get it right. There's nothing more painful than meaningless work. When asked to push a big rock up a tall mountain day after day, people stop caring and simply give up. This is no more true than in the world of sales. Daily call sessions, outbound email, repeated rejection, and the constant pressure to sell, sell, sell becomes old quickly, if … if there's no meaning at the top of that mountain, no reason for pushing a big rock up there.

Once you've established an authentic, trusting relationship with your salespeople, the next motivational essential is unleashing their unique passion. Again, I must emphasize how important it is for trust to come first before anything else in your leadership toolbox. Apart from trust, salespeople won't tell you what's going on inside because they're convinced you'll use it to manipulate them. And no one wants their own private emotions used as a weapon against them.

But the opposite is true as well. When your salespeople trust you, they'll openly tell you what makes them tick and allow you to use it to help them become the best version of their sales selves. Or, in the words of Victor Frankl in *Man's Search for Meaning*, "Those who have a 'why' to live, can bear with almost any 'how'."[3]

Here's how to unleash the why of the people who sell for you:

Purpose and Vision

Purpose and vision are two powerful leadership motivators. The two terms, often used interchangeably, are very different from each other.

Purpose is aspirational. It's a mission, a cause, a reason for being that's inspirational and ongoing. In one sense, a person never completes their purpose. How could you say, for example, that you've achieved perfect health, and now you're done with that? You've fulfilled this purpose and can scratch it off your list. No, health is an ongoing objective, an aspirational mission that always challenges us to be our best.

Vision is different. You actually complete a vision. It's a specific target, a measurable goal. Challenging, yes, but achievable. Purpose is our north star. It's a fixed point that guides our path. But we never arrive at the north star, do we? We do, however, arrive at the top of a mountain guided by the north star. The top of the mountain is the measurable vision we set for our path and the view we enjoy when we get there.

So, if your ongoing purpose is to be healthy and fit, you may choose a variety of mountains to climb: a marathon, a cross country cycling trip, or a hike on the Pacific Crest Trail. While the vision part of being healthy changes in what you do and how you do it, your purpose doesn't. Purpose outlasts vision and energizes it, but vision gives purpose the practical expression it needs to turn mere theory into reality. This is how these two dynamics complement each other.

PURPOSE	VISION
Ongoing, aspirational mission	Challenging, measurable goal
An inspiring cause	*An achievable target*
Outlives the target	Energizes the cause
Being healthy and fit	*Running a marathon*

Purpose, Vision, and Sales

When your salespeople trust you, they'll freely discuss the purpose they have for their lives and the places they see that purpose taking them, their vision. I've found over the years that people choose sales as a career for four distinct reasons: fortune, fame, freedom, and family.

For some, not most but some, the primary reason they sell is to make lots of money. They did the math, and the math of a different kind of job didn't make any sense to them. If they're going to spend fifty hours a week at work, they might as well be making the most money they can possibly make in that time. Their W2—and the things their W2 lets them buy—is the wind beneath their wings. Not very romantic, but that's what motivates some salespeople. And that's okay.

For other salespeople, much more than are willing to admit, it's not about the money. It's about what the money means. That's what I refer to as fame. Not becoming a media darling but receiving personal attention and public recognition. They love being on top of the leaderboard, being awarded prizes in front of their peers, and being praised by their supervisors. Sure, the money's fine, but many sellers are more motivated by being seen as a superstar because of the status that star power gives them.

Freedom is also something the money means for some. These people sell not for public recognition, but for the autonomy it provides. First, they can't imagine having a job that would require them to sit in a cubicle away from the rest of the world eight or more hours a day. Being out and about—on sales calls, making presentations, traveling to new places—is part of the freedom they crave at work

Neither can these people imagine a life without weekends, holidays, and lots of vacation. Plenty of sales reps have exciting outside interests they want to pursue. Selling provides both the money and the time to pursue them. This is especially true for a new generation of salespeople—gifted, talented millennials, who would much rather be given an extra week of vacation than an expensive prize they don't really care about.

Finally, some salespeople sell for family. There are those who pursue the profession because that's what will help them buy their first house, put their kids through college, support a sick spouse, or help an aging parent. Again, money is part of this equation, but it's not the most important part. The money serves a bigger purpose of heart and home.

Vision, then, flows out of purpose. In the examples above, the purpose of family drives the vision of buying a salesperson's first house or paying for their kids' college. I've had salespeople post a picture of the exact car they want to buy or a picture of the exotic vacation they want to take on the mirror in their master bathroom or on their computer monitor. When they exceed goal, that's what they're going to do with the money. Vision at work.

Vision could also be professional. While I prefer uncovering a more personal vision because it more deeply connects with our emotions, there was a time in my life when what motivated me most was career advancement. And that, too, is okay. Have that conversation with your salespeople and help them get where they want to go, whether it means becoming a sales manager or the CEO of their own company.

"What if a person's vision leads them away from your company?"

I've been asked this question more than a few times. Here's how I answer it: with another question. What would you rather have, a salesperson working half-heartedly for you hanging on for the time when they can leave and do what they really want, or a salesperson that's giving 100% effort 100% of the time to get them to the place where they can do what they really want? I will always take the latter and have found that many times in the process, a hard-working salesperson falls in love with their sales career and doesn't leave after all.

The Motivation Matrix

I've created a simple tool to talk through as a leader to uncover a salesperson's passion. It explores an individual's primary and secondary purpose and then explores his or her long-term vision for a year or more, as well as the specific steps of action this individual needs to take within the year to achieve that vision.

The Motivation Matrix

PURPOSE: Primary	PURPOSE: Secondary
What is this person's primary purpose in sales? Fortune, fame, freedom, or family?	What is this person's secondary purpose in sales? Fortune, fame, freedom, or family?
VISION: Long Term	VISION: Short Term
What is a big tangible dream this person wants to achieve?	What will move this person closer to achieving that dream every quarter, every month, every week, every day?

A digital version of this matrix is available online at
www.billzipp.com/salessuccess.

Technically speaking, vision only applies to the long term and not the short-term time frame. In other words, the phrase "short-term vision" is an oxymoron. But I use it anyway because I want to emphasize how vision fuels action. That is, the dream of running a marathon at a target time drives weekly workout habits of intervals, tempo runs, core exercises, and long runs. The same is true in sales.

Here's the bottom line: the how of sales is hard. The daily grind of prospecting, presentations, proposals, and rejections can deplete even the most dedicated rep. So, the how of sales needs a why, a very personal why that lights a fire within the soul of the people who sell for you. Strike that match and pour gasoline on it. Soon you'll have a raging inferno.

Questions, Questions, Questions

Here are some questions I've been asked in the course of presenting these principles to sales managers around the world.

1. How do you have these conversations?

So, I'm guessing that you can't see yourself saying, "What's your primary and secondary purpose in sales?" Am I right? I agree with you.

The words I use in the Motivation Matrix are not to be repeated by rote, just like you wouldn't interrogate a prospect about the details of his business by robotically reading from a list. Purpose and vision are concepts to bring up naturally and casually, exploring them over multiple conversations.

Again, these conversations take place best, as with any conversation, when there's an authentic, trusting relationship in place. But don't wait for that relationship to be perfect, either. Most of the feedback I receive from leaders who've used the Motivation Matrix is that salespeople are amazed when their managers take the time to really get to know them and find out what makes them tick. The very conversation, done well, is a powerful motivator.

2. Does purpose change over time?

Yes, purpose can change over time. I've found when salespeople first enter the workforce, fortune and fame tend to be their driving purposes. They may have school loans to pay off or expensive toys they always wanted to buy. They may also enjoy the attention they receive for winning contests and making club. Then very often, not always but often enough, as sales professionals settle in, they look for deeper meaning. Money still matters, but so does marriage and children, parents and family. In this stage of life, they tend to value time off, freedom to start the weekend early and travel the world. As a wise leader, be alert to those shifts in purpose. Don't assume the same why will work all the time. Stay close to your people and attuned to their individual motivations.

3. What if a person doesn't have a long-term vision for their life?

Many salespeople, just like many people in general, haven't thought through the concept of long-term life vision. Or they may not be in a place where answering that question makes sense for them. What do you do then? You find something, anything, that can be a personal, inspirational goal for the year.

I was sitting in on a one-on-one where a dedicated sales manager was asking about the long-term vision of the salesperson who was meeting with us. He tried asking once, and twice, and then a third time—all naturally and conversationally—but she came up blank every time.

This was a person who was hired into her first sales role six months earlier, came out of the chute extremely strong, and then began to fade. Finally, the manager asked, "Well, is there anything you want to do at the end of the year when you hit your goals?"

Her answer floored us. She had always wanted to take her friends to a Britney Spears concert in Las Vegas. Not just the concert, though, but the whole VIP experience. Front row seats, backstage passes, and all-night parties—the works. Now to be honest, neither my sales manager friend nor I would be caught dead at a Brittany Spears concert. But that's not the point, is it? The point is that idea was what motivated this young sales professional, not us. So we ran with it, and Britney Spears became her why for the year. This talented sales rep popped out of her slump and crushed her number. And oops, did it again (groan) the next year.

When your salespeople trust you as a leader, they'll open up to you about the things that matter most to them. And they'll let you use those things to motivate them to be the best version of their sales selves. You've sparked a fire within, and that's not easy to do. Congratulations! It's time now to pour gas on that fire and let it grow into a raging inferno. Enter positive praise.

Real Work Alert

I've seen hundreds of sales managers transform their leadership by asking the questions in the Motivation Matrix above. These conversations are usually conducted over time but almost always ends with the words, "Wow, I never knew that!" To help you unleash the passion of your salespeople, complete the worksheet below:

Salesperson's Name	Date	Biggest Motivational Insight
1		
2		
3		
4		
5		
6		
7		
8		

**A digital version of this worksheet is available online at
www.billzipp.com/salessuccess.**

Chapter Four
PRAISE

The salespeople who work for you are different than any other kind of employee. I know I'm stating the obvious, but it must be said anyway.

In addition, the sales profession is different than any other profession. Again, stating the obvious, but we tend to minimize these differences when it comes to leading the sales side of the business. Especially when it comes to understanding the role positive praise has in motivating salespeople to do their best work.

Wired for Praise

Most salespeople are wired for praise because of their tendency to extroversion. As I'm sure you know, the terms extroversion and introversion don't refer to being shy or outgoing. Rather, these terms refer to how a person gets their energy, which in turn, drives shy or outgoing behavior.

I'm an extrovert. I get my energy from being in front of groups, the larger the better, and being with people, the more the merrier. My wife is an introvert, and while she, like me, spends the majority of her time professionally teaching and coaching others, it doesn't give her energy as it does me. I can't get enough of the limelight. The limelight exhausts her. So after a full day of teaching, she wants to sit quietly on the couch and vegetate. I want to go to a party. We get our energy from two completely different sources, one from inside ourselves and the other from outside ourselves, and we act differently as a result.

Again, most salespeople—not all but most—get their energy from outside of themselves and need consistent positive praise, or external energy, to do their best work. This is the sales persona. An engineer does not have the same persona. A constant flow of positive praise is likely to exhaust most engineers who would prefer to be left alone in silence.

Another dynamic of the sales persona is this: While we may appear strong and confident on the outside, many of us struggle with inner doubts and insecurities on the inside. Very often, our bright public face hides darker, more difficult emotions, which again, need consistent doses of positive praise to counteract.

The sales profession is also wired for praise, not just the sales persona. Salespeople call on prospects who want to avoid them and customers who want to replace them (or at least get a better deal from them). They do their work against aggressive competitors who want to beat them and earn their compensation, either whole or in part, from the commission they receive from dealing with these prospects, customers, and competitors on a daily basis.

Sales is like riding a bicycle … uphill … with the wind in your face … all day, every day. It's hard work. Positive praise is like having a sales leader riding beside you and cheering you on. It's what gives you inspiration to get up the hill and win the race.

Here's how to do it well.

Four Pathways to Positive Praise

There are four key components, or pathways, to providing this kind of praise to the members of your sales team.

Pathway One: Be Truthful

I usually get a fair amount of pushback when I present on this topic, and the pushback goes like this, "What do I do, start making stuff up?" No, I'm not suggesting that you start making stuff up. That's called lying. Neither am I suggesting that you start giving away participation trophies. That's just stupid.

What I am suggesting, though, is that you start acting more like a coach than a cop. The role of a cop is to catch people doing things wrong and penalize them for it. A police officer doesn't pull someone over on the freeway and thank them for driving the speed limit and give them a freeway participation trophy. That's not her job. Her job is law *enforcement*.

Enforcement, however, is not a sales leader's job. Occasionally we have to enforce some mandate from on high, but these times should be rare. Most of what effective sales leaders do is build trust, unleash passion, and provide helpful instruction: inner motivation not external enforcement.

This involves catching people doing things right, not catching them doing things wrong. That's what a good coach does. A good coach looks for what is going well and then affirms the heck out of it. In doing so, they get more of the good they want. Being truthful, then, means being alert and attentive. Changing the way you see people, finding things that are good about them, and calling those things out.

They're there. You've just got to start looking for them.

Pathway Two: Be Specific

The second pathway to positive praise is being specific. Or, stated in the negative, don't make stuff up (Pathway One) and don't be a thoughtless backslapper (Pathway Two).

Don't just say, "Great job," but say, "Great job getting an appointment with that prospect. He's been impossible to nail down and you did it. Terrific work!"

Don't just say, "Thank you," but say, "Thank you for being willing to jump in and help with implementation on the new account. I know that was above and beyond the call of duty, but it saved the day for us."

Don't just say, "Congratulations," but say, "Congratulations on making club for the third year in a row. Few salespeople have that kind of consistency and tenacity. I'm proud to have you on my team."

Yes, I know, the second part of each of the statements above require more time and attention, but the return you'll get from each is more than worth it. Much more! In fact, I've seen the exact opposite occur when only the first part of each statement is offered up as praise. Salespeople roll their eyes at clueless managers who do this, revealing to the world that they have no idea how hard sales is and what salespeople actually do.

Specific praise is powerful because it identifies that precise attitudes and actions you appreciate, and by calling them out in a positive way, reinforces their likelihood of being repeated over and over again.

Pathway Three: Be Consistent

The third pathway to positive praise is being consistent. In a recent survey, the U.S. Department of Labor discovered that 69% of the American workforce did not receive any praise or recognition for the work they'd done in the last year. You read that right. Over two-thirds of employees haven't been praised in a *year*. It's like we're saying to our people, "I told you I loved you when I hired you. If that changes, I'll let you know."

The answer to this is not throwing a party every day for the people who work for you. That's not realistic, nor expected. The answer, as advised by the Gallup Corporation, is getting into a weekly rhythm of consistent, individual affirmation. At least once, every week, connecting one-one-one with a rep and praising him or her in a truthful, specific way as in the examples above.

When I first started doing this as a sales manager, it was hard to get this habit to stick. I found myself charging forward with my head down, moving onto the next week, month, quarter, and year. There were times after hours I would leave a voicemail for one (or more) of my salespeople just to make sure I got everyone checked off my list (which, by the way, is not so bad an idea. A voicemail message allows someone to listen to your words of affirmation over and over again). Soon, however, it became part of my regular mode of conversation. It can be yours as well with a little grit and determination.

Need I remind you that no complicated system is required to do this, nor do you need expensive awards programs. Just honest, thoughtful, sincere appreciation. And the best part? It's free. "Because of its power, ridiculously low cost and rarity, praise and recognition is one of the greatest lost opportunities in the business world today," write Gallup researchers Rodd Wagner and James Harter in *12: The Elements of Great Managing.*[4]

Pathway Four: Be Accountable

The fourth and final pathway to positive praise is being accountable.

To help you provide this kind of praise as a sales leader, I've created a simple worksheet that's been used hundreds, if not thousands, of times by sales leaders around the world. It's super simple to fill out. Just list the names of the people on your sales team in the left column of the worksheet and check the boxes in the right column when you give each person a piece of truthful, specific praise during the week.

Get a partner and be accountable to this person for using this worksheet four weeks in a row. Fill it out each week and check-in with each other to see how it's going. At the end of four weeks, sit down together and review the results.

The Weekly Affirmation Worksheet

Salesperson's Name	M	T	W	T	F
	☐	☐	☐	☐	☐
	☐	☐	☐	☐	☐
	☐	☐	☐	☐	☐
	☐	☐	☐	☐	☐
	☐	☐	☐	☐	☐
	☐	☐	☐	☐	☐
	☐	☐	☐	☐	☐
	☐	☐	☐	☐	☐

A digital version of this worksheet is available online at www.billzipp.com/salessuccess.

When you accept this accountability challenge, you'll experience two distinct things with the worksheet. The first thing you'll experience is how generic and nonspecific your praise really is. If you honestly fill it out and only give yourself a tally when the praise you've given a salesperson is both truthful and specific, you'll be surprised at how shallow and superficial you've been in affirming other people.

The second thing you'll experience when you use this worksheet is how inconsistent you've been with *all* the members of your team. You'll discover, as I did, that it was much easier to praise some salespeople rather than others, so as a result, some salespeople receive generous doses of affirmation and others receive none.

This inevitably makes the situation worse. If you go out to a fancy restaurant for a great meal and everything goes poorly, the wait is long and the food is cold, the only thing that could make that worse is if the waitstaff ignores you and pretends that nothing's wrong. I've been in situations like that and it's infuriating. But I've also had waitstaff apologize profusely, bring extra bread, keep the beer flowing, and comp dessert. In the end, we were treated so wonderfully that we forgot how bad the meal had actually been.

So think of that person (or persons) on your team who you're avoiding. Is your lack of attention making the situation better or worse? I'm guessing worse, right? So start being consistent with your praise to everyone, every week.

Positive Praise Won't Work When...

As important and as powerful as positive praise is, there's one thing it is not: a cure-all. Effective sales leadership is not as easy as taking a positivity pill or waving a magic wand at people. Positive praise must complement other tools in a sales leader's toolbox and work together with them to get the job done. Stated in another way, positive praise does not work when the following conditions exist:

1. Positive praise won't work when you're looking for a quick fix.

Imagine turning sixty-five years old and deciding for the first time in your life to start saving for retirement. How much money will you be able to set aside? Financial experts would all agree—not much. The way to save for retirement is little by little, month by month, over the course of years. Interest compounds and equity builds, not by one heroic act of savings, but by hundreds of small investments.

When we as leaders realize that we have set a negative tone for our team and make the commitment to delivering positive praise on a regular basis, we must view it as long-term investment. One great act of affirmation at a team meeting or a year-end banquet will only go so far. Like starting to save for retirement at sixty-five, a quick fix approach to praise does not build up the kind of equity that is needed to be effective with people. This is true for any leadership behavior, not just this one. Great leadership is a cloth with many threads of action woven consistently over time.

The good news is that you can start immediately and make a real difference. And although the emotional bank account of many of your salespeople might be overdrawn, you'll be surprised at how quickly you can bring it back into balance again. Relationships are resilient and people respond well when their leaders make a genuine, consistent effort to do the right thing.

2. Positive praise won't work when you need to apologize first.

We've all experienced this. A person crosses the line and offends us. You know it. They know it. And everyone else knows it too. But instead of coming to us and saying they're sorry, this person treats us differently. They're sugary sweet and sickeningly nice, never mentioning a word about the offense.

Positive praise will not work when an apology needs to be made first. In fact, just the opposite will happen. Praise will be seen as hollow and manipulative, just another withdrawal in a long list of withdrawals and cowardly avoidance of the real heart issue at hand. If you've made an honest mistake, or if you've really blown it with another person, admit it. Apologize and move on. Don't cover it up like a fresh coat of paint on rotten wood, pretending everything will be okay. Everything won't be okay. That's not the way paint, or praise, works. Say you're sorry. Own your mistake, openly, honestly, and humbly.

3. Positive praise won't work when it's the only communication tool you use.

There's an interesting corollary to the five positive comments to every one negative comment ratio we've all heard about. Researchers found that when positive comments to negative comments exceeded ten to one or more, workplace productivity actually decreased.[5] In other words, you can praise too much, never delivering other important kinds of communication.

Yes, praise creates a climate where people feel empowered, but it's not the only thing that does. Empowerment also occurs when we instruct, explain, dialogue, debate, question, challenge, and correct. Yes, some of these things will make withdrawals—actually most of them will—but that's okay. When we make enough praise deposits with our salespeople, the relationship will be fine.

4. Positive praise won't work when talent is misaligned to task.

A bird is born to fly. A fish is born to swim. The talent for the task is present in them, and, as result, they complete these activities. Salespeople are born to sell. That is, somewhere in their soul is the raw DNA—the natural drive—for selling. The point, then, of praise is not to motivate them to do something they really don't want to do but to motivate them to do it better.

Sure, there may be times where a swimming animal may be rewarded for jumping out of the water and "flying," or a flying animal may be rewarded for diving into the water and "swimming," but it's short-lived. These animals will always return to their natural environment. You can curse or cajole someone who's not built for sales into selling more. But it will be always be short-lived because talent is not aligned to task.

If you praise and praise and praise someone and see no increase in performance, or just a short-term spike in the number, you don't have a praise problem. You have a fit problem. No amount of praise will fix a fit problem, because you can't put in what God left out. It's time for a different conversation, albeit an uncomfortable one. It's a conversation about a better professional alignment of talent to task. I've had my share of these, and I know they're not easy to pull off. Without exception, however, they've ended up being in the best interests of both the sales organization and the struggling salesperson.

Want to Know about My Best Day at This Company?

I was coaching a sales leader who was making the difficult transition from individual contributor to frontline sales manager. It was not going well. He had lost another member of his team, mostly due to his abrasive leadership, and was way, way off mark for hitting goal for the year.

As we were reviewing some painful feedback, he randomly said to me, "You want to know about my best day at this company?"

"Yes," I said, open to anything that would divert us from this difficult discussion.

He had crushed his sales number and was the top salesperson in his division for the year. At the awards banquet, his boss brought him up on stage to be cheered by all his peers.

Then this brilliant leader said, "Everyone knows this is a hard job and none of us could do it without the support and sacrifice of our spouse." The salesperson's wife was brought on the platform and she received a standing ovation.

Years later, he still choked up telling the story, and it still motivated him to give his very best effort at work. That's the power of positive praise.

Real Work Alert

The third real work assignment I'm giving you is using the Weekly Affirmation Worksheet below for an entire month. Complete this activity for four straight weeks with some work colleagues to hold you accountable for getting it done (or all you'll do is get halfway through the first week and quit).

What weeks will you complete this real work assignment?

Start Date: _____

End Date: _____

Who will you do this real work with?

Colleague One: _____

Colleague Two: _____

Colleague Three: _____

WEEK ONE DATE:					
Salesperson's Name	**M**	**T**	**W**	**T**	**F**
	☐	☐	☐	☐	☐
	☐	☐	☐	☐	☐

	M	T	W	T	F
	☐	☐	☐	☐	☐
	☐	☐	☐	☐	☐
	☐	☐	☐	☐	☐
	☐	☐	☐	☐	☐
	☐	☐	☐	☐	☐
	☐	☐	☐	☐	☐

WEEK TWO DATE:

Salesperson's Name	M	T	W	T	F
	☐	☐	☐	☐	☐
	☐	☐	☐	☐	☐
	☐	☐	☐	☐	☐
	☐	☐	☐	☐	☐
	☐	☐	☐	☐	☐
	☐	☐	☐	☐	☐
	☐	☐	☐	☐	☐
	☐	☐	☐	☐	☐

WEEK THREE DATE:

Salesperson's Name	M	T	W	T	F
	☐	☐	☐	☐	☐
	☐	☐	☐	☐	☐
	☐	☐	☐	☐	☐
	☐	☐	☐	☐	☐
	☐	☐	☐	☐	☐
	☐	☐	☐	☐	☐
	☐	☐	☐	☐	☐
	☐	☐	☐	☐	☐

WEEK FOUR DATE:

Salesperson's Name	M	T	W	T	F
	☐	☐	☐	☐	☐
	☐	☐	☐	☐	☐
	☐	☐	☐	☐	☐
	☐	☐	☐	☐	☐
	☐	☐	☐	☐	☐

	☐	☐	☐	☐	☐
	☐	☐	☐	☐	☐
	☐	☐	☐	☐	☐

**A digital version of this worksheet is available online at
www.billzipp.com/salessuccess.**

What did you learn about your leadership in this area during these four weeks?

What did you learn about your salespeople during these four weeks?

How can you make positive praise a consistent habit every week of the year?

Chapter Five
CULTURE

I love Kmart. But not for the low, low prices or the blue light specials. I love Kmart because wherever I travel in the United States, I can find a dead plant there. Let me explain...

When I'm asked to speak on building a winning sales culture, I begin my talk by putting a dead plant in front of the audience and asking the group what this plant needs. We generate a list—water, air, nutrients in the soil, re-planting, pruning—and discuss the ways in which this list parallels the sales context.

There's one problem with that ingenious ploy, however. Where do you find a dead plant on demand? The solution ... Kmart. They've never failed to deliver. In fact, there's always a good supply of dead plants on their shelves from which to choose.

When I take my dead plant to the check-out line to pay for it, I ask the attendant if he or she could discount it for me because the plant is, obviously, quite dead. A conversation like this ensues:

"I'm sorry sir, I'm not allowed to do that."

"But the plant is dead," I reply.

"It's not our policy to discount dead plants. Then everyone would want them."

"And that would be a problem? The plant is dead!"

"That'll be $10.99, sir."

I shake my head in wonder at the irony of this situation, especially given Kmart's recent performance in the marketplace.

A Winning Sales Culture

I've learned a lot over the last few decades asking the dead plant question about what it takes to build a winning sales culture. I've come to see the answer to that question as being one of the most important priorities to attend to in sales leadership.

The stark reality is this. You may have the best product at the best price. You may have the most brilliant sales strategy being executed by the most talented sales staff. You may have the latest cutting-edge technology and the slickest social media presence, but if your culture is broken, all of that stuff—every bit of it—is dead on arrival. Or in the words of Peter Drucker, "Culture eats strategy for breakfast!"[6]

What is Culture?

Simply stated, culture is the combination of beliefs and behaviors any group of people embrace, from businesses to churches, families to nations. It's the way these people think and the way they act in these groups consistently over time. Culture drives the way we work as a team, the way we treat our customers, the way we pursue our goals, and the way we respond to adversity.

Culture is the one thing that changes everything. It's the undercurrent of all that goes on in your sales organization and the riptide that can drown any initiative that drifts into its path. Which makes building a winning sales culture one of your top priorities as a leader. And that means changing the way people think and act, from your top leaders to your frontline staff. What does a winning sales culture look like? I'm glad you asked. Here are its four fundamentals:

A Winning Sales Culture is Based on Mutual Respect

The first fundamental for a winning sales culture is the nature of the relationships in it. Here, again, is where *who* comes before *why* or *what*, the *who* being how sales leaders and sales representatives view and treat one another.

Note those words, in that order: view and treat. Many times we try to get people to treat others with respect without addressing how they think about that person or group of people. This is fatally flawed. Behavior flows from belief, how one acts is shaped by how one thinks. Respect begins between the ears, then finds its external expression.

How do *you* think about your salespeople? Leaders who create a winning sales culture don't view their sales staff as interchangeable parts but as unique human beings worthy of dignity and respect. They see themselves as a first among equals, not higher or lower than the people they lead. They don't assume the worst when things go wrong and believe the best in others.

Yes, I know, not everyone will live up to these high expectations. But most will, and that's worth the risk for me in thinking this way about them. For those who don't live up, I can look myself in the mirror and know that I believed the best in them until they gave me no other alternative.

That's how leaders who build a winning sales culture think. Here's how they act. They speak with respect to the people who report to them, never demeaning them outside of their presence or behind their back. They give others the credit they deserve, fully and completely, and accept blame themselves. And they insist others do as well.

Leaders building a winning sales culture correct with respect. When a salesperson makes a mistake, which most every salesperson finds a way to do, that conversation is conducted in private, not in public, refusing to humiliate this person in front of his or her peers. Conversely, when a sales leader makes a mistake, which most every sales leader finds a way to do, apologies are done in public, displaying the authenticity and vulnerability that engenders respect.

Respect is like offering someone a handshake. Only the rare individual will refuse to shake your hand. When you offer respect in the manner described above, your salespeople will respond to the gesture and give you respect in the return. Then they'll reach out to others on your team and shake their hands as well. That's how a winning sales culture is built, one handshake at a time.

A Winning Sales Culture is Driven by Grit and Determination

Grit, true grit that is, has a formal definition. Not the one given by the 1969 movie where John Wayne won his only Academy Award or by the recent Coen brothers' remake. The grit young Mattie Ross found in the aging "Rooster" Cogburn was an ability to stand up to bad guys and shoot a gun. Important, maybe, in the wild, wild west, but not helpful for today's business marketplace.

So Dr. Angela Duckworth and her research team at the University of Pennsylvania have performed an incredible service by giving us this succinct—and profoundly useful—definition. True grit is "passion and perseverance for long-term goals."[7] Grit is courage, not just in the moment but sustained over time, in the ongoing pursuit of challenging goals. According to research, this kind of grit outperforms both talent and intelligence in activities as diverse as graduating from military school and competing in the National Spelling Bee.

Passion and perseverance for long-term goals describes the sales role almost perfectly. Every year a sales person chases a number, their long-term goal, and is compensated for actually hitting that number (or not). Then they do it again the next year. And the next. And the next. Passion for this pursuit comes from the factors we discussed in Chapter 2, purpose and vision, but where does perseverance come from?

Perseverance in sales comes from three sources: belief in yourself, belief in your solution, and belief in your process. These three always get it done.

The first thing you can do to hardwire perseverance in your salespeople is help them believe in themselves. Contrary to popular opinion, however, believing in one's self does not come from reciting positive platitudes over and over again (I am special! I am a success! I am a sales snowflake!). It comes from producing positive outcomes. True self-esteem flows from self-efficacy, the ability to act on one's own behalf to achieve challenging goals.

So get rid of the pop culture psycho-babble that seeps into sales and get serious about actually helping people succeed. A hard-won deal is infinitely better for a person's self-image than an inspirational poster or motivational quote. When you give your sellers the real help they need to win, along with the win you'll get something even better: the confidence that comes from competence and the birth of a winning sales culture.

The second source of perseverance is believing in your solution. You and your salespeople have to believe that the product or service you bring to the marketplace does what it says it will do, improving the customer's condition. Not that it's a perfect product or service, nothing is perfect this side of eternity. Not that it's the best product or service either, not everyone can afford a Lexus or a BMW. Some of us have to drive a Camry. But, say it with me, "it does what it says it will do."

Here again is where sales departs from other business activities: it's a highly personal profession. Salespeople put their reputation on the line every time they seek to sell something and deserve to have that risk backed by actual results. If you can't guarantee reasonable results for the people who sell for you, it's time for both of you to find a new company to represent.

The third source of perseverance is belief in your sales process. According to logistics experts, manufacturing mistakes occur 85% of the time due to non-human errors in the system. And while that percentage seems a bit high to me, there is a tendency to point to people and not the process when things break down. The same is true in sales.

Now, there's no perfect sales process. I've never seen one in decades of doing this work. But it is possible to have a reliable sales process, one that's been tested and proven over time. One that you and your people can believe in, follow, and win.

If that's not true about your sales process, become an army of one to make improvements to it. And keep making improvements until it becomes as reliable as turning on water in the shower. Then make more improvements to it, because the marketplace is ever changing. Nothing fails like success! Your salespeople, who put their livelihood on the line for you day after day, deserve this kind of diligence.

A Winning Sales Culture is Infused with a Sense of Fun and Play

There's a second—and opposite—set of emotions from the drive of grit and determination: a sense of fun and play. Yes, I know it's an odd thing to say in a serious sales leadership book, but fun and play are essential to creating a winning sales culture. Why? Because human emotions exist in an open-loop system.

We're all familiar with a closed-loop system. The transmission in our car or the veins in our bodies are examples of a closed-loop system. They run in a self-regulating manner and aren't designed to accept outside influences. If they do, something bad happens.

Human emotions aren't like that at all. They're easily affected by outside influences. Negative emotions spread like a cold, making everyone sick and sour. Positive emotions do the same but with opposite results. That's why fun and play is an important business priority. It fans the flame of positive emotions and pours water on negative ones. It brings oxygen into the room and lets people breathe.

When I speak to a group of sales leaders, I can immediately tell how well they're doing by the mood of the group. Is it tense? Troubled? Or do the leaders laugh readily, tease each other in good humor, and genuinely enjoy working together?

"Understanding the powerful role of emotions in the workplace sets the best leaders apart from the rest," declares Daniel Goleman in *Primal Leadership*, "not just in tangibles such as better business results and the retention of top talent, but also in the all-important intangibles, such as higher morale, motivation, and commitment."[8]

How do you infuse a sense of play in your sales culture?

First, make fun of yourself. Let people laugh at you in a self-depreciating way. Be the punchline to your own jokes. Second, celebrate things that aren't sales related: birthdays, graduations, St. Patrick's Day, whatever. Find any stupid excuse to throw a party or have a cake. The stupider the better. Third, do things together. Fun things. Super fun things. The best team-building event I ever participated in was a *WhirlyBall* tournament after a sales leadership development day in downtown Chicago. Yes, *WhirlyBall* is a thing. Google it. It was awesome!

A Winning Sales Culture Blends Both Humanity and Honesty

One of the best business book I've read is *Radical Candor* by Kim Scott, a leadership veteran at both Google and Apple. The book begins, however, with a gripping story from Kim's own start-up. She had been dragging her feet in letting go an underperforming employee. When she did, he blurted out, "Why didn't you tell me? Why didn't *anyone* tell me? I thought you all cared about me?"[9]

The echoes of this question sent Kim on a quest for a new model of communication for all of her workplace relationships, not just underperforming employees. She calls that model radical candor, which is a perfect blend of caring personally for your people and challenging them directly. *Radical Candor* states that if you care personally for people but avoid challenging them directly, you'll become "ruinously sympathetic." Conversely, if you challenge people directly but don't care for them personally, you'll become "obnoxiously aggressive."

Neither option works.

The words I use for this concept are being human and being honest. And yes, it's one concept and not two, because both are needed *at the same* time to build a winning sales culture. The very best sales leaders put their arms around their salespeople and tell them how much they love them. Then they poke them in the ribs, and keep poking them, to help their reps become the best version of themselves.

The hug alone—that is, being human—won't do it because all human beings, not just salespeople, need someone outside of themselves to help them be their very best. But, of course, pokes alone won't work either, because without a metaphorical hug, brutal honesty is counterproductive. It's like saying, "The beatings will stop when morale improves!" Well, how's that going to happen? This is why Kim chose the words ruinously sympathetic and obnoxiously aggressive to describe these two extremes.

Sales leaders I've worked with over the years tend to fall off one side of the balance beam on this or the other. Some are nice but never hit their number. Others hit their number but aren't nice (known by all to be a jerk). You're not condemned to live in either of these two extremes. If your tendency is to be nice, don't stop being nice. Lean into your discomfort and learn how to be candid and forthright. If your tendency is just the opposite, don't stop being honest, learn how to care for your people and show compassion, lean into your shared humanity.

Two Culture Building Tools

Now that we've identified the components of a winning sales culture, how do you go about building one? There are two tools you can use to do this: stories and artifacts.

Telling Good Stories

For millennia, the human race has told stories. Cultural traditions have been passed down by tribal elders telling fables around the fire and doting mothers telling bedtime tales. Storytelling is the single-most powerful way to build a winning sales culture as well. That's why I use so many in my writing and speaking. I've had people come up to me years after hearing me present somewhere and retell me one of my crazy stories.

This happens because there's something magical about a story. It connects with people in a way that mere bullet points in a slide deck never do. It embodies those bullet points in real flesh and blood and reinforces the behavior you're trying to build in your sales team when other people tell and retell the story. It also celebrates the hero of the story, usually one of your reps, doubling as positive praise. In other words, instead of challenging embedded behavior and beliefs head-on through a locked and bolted front door, a well-told story sneaks in the back door and hits people over the head with a two-by-four when they're not looking.

Good storytelling is simple, but it's not easy. Here's a basic template to follow:

1. Set the Context

The very first thing to do in telling a good story is immediately set the context. In a brief sentence or two, transport the audience from where they are now to an entirely different time and place. This is done by stating clearly and concisely the *when*, *who*, and *where* of the story. Don't mess with that formula: *when*, *who*, and *where* must be done in that exact order for maximum impact.

2. State the Conflict

The next thing to do in telling a good story is to create conflict. Without conflict, there is no story, just empty words. State the conflict by presenting a pressing problem, which on the surface, does not appear to have any solution. A pressing problem with no apparent solution is the very definition of conflict.

3. Divulge the Details

Once the context of your story is set and conflict created, you've bought yourself some time. You've hooked your listeners and can use that hook to deliver the details needed for the story to develop and have meaningful impact. Details add color that make the story feel real and establish a platform of authority for what you're going to conclude from it. Don't drown your audience in details, however. Every piece of minutiae that happened does not have to be recounted, just the stuff that's relevant to the conflict and the point.

4. Resolve the Conflict (Or Not)

Now resolve the conflict, or don't resolve it. Good stories come in two flavors: comedy and tragedy. The comedy is a story that has resolution to the conflict. The tragedy is a story where the conflict doesn't have resolution and negative consequences occur. You can go either way on this with your stories; both work well—gain or loss, pleasure or pain.

5. Make the Point

Here's the payoff, the point of the story you're telling. With a comedy, describe in detail the new reality that exists because a solution to the pressing problem was discovered. Don't just simply conclude, "And they all lived happily ever after," or something generic like that. Drive your point home by specifically stating how the solution created a completely new reality for the people in the story.

For a tragedy, when the conflict is unresolved, take a different tack. Present the moral to the story, the lesson that must be learned from the unnecessary loss. When I make a point in my stories, I like to use a brief but powerful quote to sum things up. Look at how I did that at the beginning of this chapter with the Kmart story and a quote from Peter Drucker.

Here are six stories you should be able to tell as a sales leader:

- The story of a new sales rep and how she got to quota faster than anyone else in the company
- The story of a seasoned sales rep who slipped into a slump and then pulled himself out of his slump, making club for the third year in a row
- The story of a struggling business who adopted your product (or service) and experienced a whole new level of success

- The story of a struggling business who didn't adopt your product (or service) and continued to struggle, ultimately going out of business
- The story of a sales rep whose deal fell apart in implementation, but she kept working on it internally and externally until the account became her biggest customer
- The story of a sales rep who couldn't get a meeting with a target prospect but found a shared contact on LinkedIn and used that contact to secure a first appointment that ultimately brought in lots of business

Using Memorable Artifacts

In addition to good stories, memorable artifacts are also a key to building a winning sales culture. Artifacts is an odd word to use related to sales culture. We tend to think about an artifact as something discovered in an archaeological dig—you know, *Indiana Jones and the Temple of Doom*. But think about it. An archaeological artifact is an object that reflects the activities and values of an ancient culture.

A living culture, like the one you're building right now, also has objects that reflect its activities and values, and these artifacts create powerful, symbolic connections in the soul of your sellers. These memorable artifacts fall into two categories: old-school and new-school.

New school artifacts, unlike old-school artifacts, aren't physical objects but digital ones. A photo on Instagram, a video on YouTube, a post on Facebook, or a shout-out on Twitter all land in this bucket. And because most everyone is going new-school, the more classic pins and plaques, jewelry and clothing have made a comeback. Use both liberally to express the respect you have for your sales team, to celebrate grit and determination, to infuse a sense of fun and play into what you do, and to communicate with humanity and honesty.

We all love a good app, don't we? It may be a game, a social media site, a to-do list manager, or a news aggregator. We have our favorites and use them every day, many times a day. No app in the world, however, can make up for a bad operating system. If the operating system on your smartphone is slow, out of date, or simply broken beyond repair, no app will work, no matter how amazing it is.

Simply stated, culture is the operating system at the heart of your sales operation. If you're going to succeed in this leadership role, building a winning sales culture must become one of your top priorities.

PART II
MOBILIZATION

"Coaching is the single most important part of expanding others' capabilities. It's the difference between giving orders and teaching people how to get things done. Good leaders regard every encounter as an opportunity to coach."[10]

—**Larry Bossidy** and **Ram Charan**

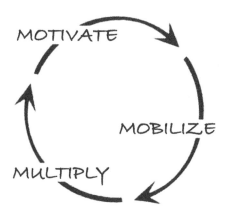

Chapter Six

GOALS

Most sales leaders get goals all wrong. Because the sales environment is defined by setting a target for revenue generation by the end of the year and working back from that target, measuring progress every month, sales leaders assume they've got goals down.

And they do, to a degree. But to a minimal degree.

While having revenue numbers is a start when it comes to setting sales goals, it's just a start and people will fail miserably if these numbers are the only kind of goals a sales leader sets with their reps. Let me explain…'

Target Time and Weekly Workouts

Five years ago, due to an incredible lack of personal judgment, I registered to run a half-marathon. I'd been running races for a while,

5Ks and 10Ks, but had never competed at this distance before. It seemed like a fun thing to do at the time (it was more challenging than I ever thought), so I signed up for the race, paid the fee, and got to work.

The first thing I did was set the target time I would run my half marathon in. Through a purely scientific process—insert personal pride here—I landed on two hours and fifteen minutes. I put the number 2:15 on a bunch of three-by-five cards and taped them all over the place, the bathroom mirror, my computer monitor, and the dashboard of my car. You get the idea.

But I also did something else. I hired a coach. My coach met with me, took down all the information about my health and running history, and asked me about my target time. She then did what I hired her to do. She created a weekly workout plan, which would prepare me to achieve my target time.

The plan involved long runs and short runs, tempo runs and intervals. It even involved doing crunches. On Monday morning, I would check-in with my coach, tell her how the week went, and she would adjust the plan, making some things easier and other things harder. We did this every week for almost twenty weeks.

Race day came, a wonderfully cool and cloudy day in Oregon. Perfect marathon weather! I ran the race in 2:15:37, fading only slightly at the end.

Performance Goals and Process Goals

This experience, and the role of my coach in helping me in it, is the secret to setting goals with your salespeople. Target time is like quota, the ultimate number your rep needs to hit by the end of the year. It's not irrelevant, but it's not enough. It's a performance goal.

What's also needed, however, are process goals. Weekly workouts. The specific plan that needs to be followed to achieve a target time (or a sales quota). It's what a rep, like any long-distance runner, needs to do every day of every week to have a healthy, robust pipeline: number of outbound contacts, first appointments, executive overviews, proposal presentations, and the like.

And here is where most sales leaders get goals all wrong. They beat the drum of quota over and over again. They put that number on three-by-five cards, or their digital equivalent, and post it everywhere. Then they wonder why people don't hit it. That would be like me preparing for the half marathon by repeating aloud, "2:15 … 2:15 … 2:15 … 2:15."

Ridiculous, right?

All performance goals need process goals so they become reality. That means, like my running coach did, sitting down with each of your reps, understanding their sales development history, creating a weekly sales workout plan, checking in on that plan every Monday morning, and adjusting it accordingly.

This, and only this, is how sales goals really work.

Sales Performance Goals	Sales Process Goals
Total sales by month, quarter, and year	Sales activities by day, week, and month
Accomplished and re-set each year	*Repeated over and over again*
What your salespeople need to achieve	**How** your salespeople can achieve it
Target marathon time	*Weekly running workouts*

Sales Process Insight

This compels me to ask you another question. How well do you know your sales process so you can actually create meaningful process goals?

My running coach knew the process behind preparing for marathons, half and full. She had run plenty herself and helped hundreds of runners just like me do the same. When she created my weekly workout plans, she used this knowledge to determine just how long my long runs should be and also how short my recovery runs should be. Each week she told me just how fast my tempo runs should be and how many intervals, at what distance and what pace, I should repeat. She even told me how many crunches I should do (I *hate* crunches. But more on that later). All of these were designed to help me achieve my target time. Again, that time was not irrelevant, but it was not enough.

Have you broken down the sales process of your company into the specific, repeated activities your salespeople need to do every day of every week? In two decades of consulting, I've found this kind of clarity to be rare among sales leaders. Most managers act as cheerleaders on the sideline chanting, "Just sell, baby!" and wonder why their reps just don't.

What do sales process goals look like? Let me take you behind the scenes of my own consulting firm. I work deeply with a small amount of companies each year who are seeking to increase sales performance and productivity. In a typical year, I have eighteen or so speaking, coaching, or consulting engagements. I close about two-thirds of the projects I propose, so simple math states that I need twenty-seven to thirty proposals under consideration every year, or seven to eight per quarter.

So far so good, right? One of my process goals is to have two, and sometimes three, proposal presentations a month. But what gets me those presentations? The next set of numbers are these: twenty target clients nets five or six appointments that ultimately become two or three proposals under consideration per month.

So here's my next process goal: set five to six appointments per month.

But that's not enough, because it takes four to five emails and/or phone calls to my target prospects to get those appointments scheduled on the calendar. When you do some more math, four times twenty to twenty-five is eighty to one hundred, divided by four weeks in a month, and I have another process goal: twenty to twenty-five outbound sales calls per week.

Here's what this looks like:

Performance Goal	*18 speaking, coaching, or consulting engagements per year*
Process Goals	20–25 outbound sales calls per week to target prospects
	5–6 appointments per month with target prospects
	2–3 proposal presentations per month

Few independent consultants have thought things through like this, which is why so many go out of business. I know these numbers because I've been repeating them like clockwork for two decades. They've adjusted over time, but that's the reality of my business. Like the life of any salesperson, no one's going to make these calls for me. I schedule them in my calendar and get them done, without exception.

Now look at your sales process and work backwards from a closed deal. What gets you there, specifically by calls, appointments, and presentations every quarter, month, week, and day? Anything less is sales management malpractice.

Beyond the Numbers

And of course, it's not as easy as all that. Quality of sales activity needs to be specified as well as its quantity. So, while you're breaking down your performance goals into specific repeated activities, take the time to define exactly what each activity entails.

I was asked by the CEO of a digital media company to help his salespeople close more business. He described how the sellers on his staff had huge pipelines with tons of prospects in them, but very little of that business was actually turning into done deals.

In the course of working with the company, however, I discovered the real problem. The real problem wasn't closing business but opening qualified opportunities. No one had taken the time to define what a first appointment actually looked like, so outbound emails, voice mail messages, and casual conversations at networking meetings were being entered into their CRM as actual opportunities, when in fact, they were nothing more than random relational connections. Not bad, of course, but certainly not first appointments.

So we defined a "first appointment." A first appointment is a scheduled meeting, face-to-face or over the phone, with a qualified prospect where a salesperson and that prospect talk about that company's challenges related to marketing its products and services in today's digital marketplace. Additionally, the effectiveness of these first appointments is measured by whether or not that meeting results in a second appointment at least half of the time.

Two things happened when we did this. First, their sales pipeline got very, very skinny. But that's okay because it was mostly filled with fluff anyway. Then, as these reps were equipped on how to conduct a great first appointment and were held accountable for having them, close ratios rose to 25%. Then, after we worked on improving their closing skills, they soared to almost 50%.

Here's my bottom line: Sales goals fail us not because they don't exist, but because they aren't specific enough in the way they're set.

The Science of Human Behavior Change

What we're talking about when it comes to helping our reps set and achieve sales process goals is changing human behavior, a notoriously difficult thing to do. For we are creatures of habit and tend to do things the way we've always done them, whether that way works for us or not.

For example, one of your salespeople always sends long rambling emails to prospective customers with a half dozen attachments. This bloated correspondence doesn't get opened, doesn't get read, and most certainly doesn't get a response. You've provided training to the team on how to write crisp, succinct email in one hundred words or less with a powerful value proposition and a clear call to action. But what does this rep do? He continues to send long rambling emails with a half dozen attachments, because that's what he's always done.

Why? As the law of inertia tell us, a salesperson at rest, stays at rest. And that's a problem. So here are three keys to disrupting inertia and helping your sellers become the best version of themselves:

1. Focus on Incremental Improvement

The reason why most attempts at behavior change fail is because we try to do too much too soon. That's the thesis of James Clear's brilliant book *Atomic Habits*. Contrary to the overnight success stories we hear in the press (which are over-blown anyway), *Atomic Habits* maintains that real change takes place through the "aggregation of marginal gains." Which is fancy way of saying that a thousand small things add up to one big thing.

"Habits are the compound interest of self-improvement," Clear writes. "The same way that money multiplies through compound interest, the effects of your habits multiply as you repeat them. They seem to make little difference on any given day, and yet the impact they deliver over the months and years can be enormous."[11]

Something as simple as a 1% improvement repeated each day over an entire fiscal year will yield a 38% increase in sales (37.78% to be exact). This, then, should impact the way we set process goals, breaking them down into even smaller, more marginal steps of action, which a salesperson can repeat over and over again until the behavior becomes automatic and the compound interest of self-improvement multiplies in their favor.

2. Provide Immediate Reward

There's one problem with compound interest, however. It doesn't provide an immediate reward. That's why we buy a newer version of the completely serviceable car we have, rather than put more money into retirement savings. That's why we down a third beer and the rest of the pepperoni pizza, rather than push ourselves away from the table. The immediate pleasure we get *in the moment* from those actions outweighs any distant, future benefits.

So the second key to behavior change is giving attempts at developing a new habit an immediate reward until it becomes ingrained. This rewires our brain to enjoy the new behavior right away and not rely on the uncertainties of delayed gratification.

My running coach did this with me to get me to do crunches (again, which I hate). Core strength is critical for long distance runners because when your core breaks down, your upper body bends over, you breathe less deeply, and you start to shuffle down the road instead of run. At the end of most any marathon or half marathon, you'll see some poor soul whose core collapsed hobble across the finish line, bent over in agonizing pain. But that benefit was so far out in the future for me that I remained completely unmotivated to do even one crunch in my workouts. During our weekly check-ins, my coach would ask me how my crunches were going, and week after week I reported to her that I hadn't done any. So, she said to me, "Here's what I'll do, Bill. You do your crunches this week, and I'll drop one round of intervals from your interval day. Okay?"

Now intervals are the second most miserable thing you'll ever do in preparing to run a marathon, and this reward got my attention. I did my crunches. The next week, she had another reward and the week after that, another. Pretty soon I was doing crunches as a regular part of every workout.

In the sales environment, meeting goal at the end of the year and qualifying for President's Club—as cool as that is—does not provide the immediacy needed to change behavior. Being above goal at the end of the month is not immediate enough either.

If you're going to change the behavior of your salespeople, breakdown the sales activities you want them to do into small, incremental steps. Find fun, creative ways to immediately reward those steps, rewiring your reps' sales brain to make these behaviors automatic. These rewards don't need to be, and probably shouldn't be, something expensive. A shout-out at a sales meeting, a Starbucks gift card, or a Friday afternoon off, all work wonders.

3. Break the Frequency Barrier

Automatic, that's what a habit is. It's something we've done so many times that we do it without thinking, like driving to the office the same route every day or checking Facebook for no apparent reason. This is what you want as a sales leader—for the rep who sends long rambling prospecting email to write crisp, succinct ones, and to do that ten times a day, every day without giving it a second thought. When this happens, you've broken the frequency barrier with that rep.

Breaking the frequency barrier occurs when an activity has been repeated so many times that it becomes automatic. When someone breaks the frequency barrier, they've mastered a habit. It's now second nature to them.

There's a common misperception about this, however. Have you heard the claim that it takes twenty-one days to learn a new habit? That's not true. It's a myth. Somebody made it up (maybe somebody selling twenty-one-day habit planners). Yes, time is a factor in acquiring a habit, but so is repetition. Without enough repetition, no activity will become automatic, even though a twenty-one-day time period has passed.

And there's a whole other dynamic in acquiring a new habit: degree of difficulty. An extremely complex habit, like playing the violin, may take twenty-one years to master, not twenty-one days. The formula for breaking the frequency barrier, then, looks like this:

Number of **Repetitions**
multiplied over
Time
divided by
Degree of Difficulty
Equals
Habit Mastery

Inputting your code into the office security system so an alarm doesn't go off may take five repetitions over five minutes to master. Writing a succinct sales email that results in a first appointment may take hundreds of repetitions over months to master. That's how the formula works.

Use this formula to your advantage by defining in detail the activities you want your salespeople to do. Get them doing these activities as frequently as possible, providing immediate rewards along the way. Be attentive to the degree of difficulty and give your team the time it needs to master new sales skills. Now rinse and repeat.

The Danger of Breaking the Frequency Barrier

Finally, there's a danger to breaking the frequency barrier and the danger is this: complacency. When you do something automatically, you can do it without thinking, operating on autopilot. That's how mistakes are made. That's why you left your house the other day and drove to the office when you were supposed to pick the kids up from school. An automatic habit kicked in and you acted without thinking.

That's also why some of your most seasoned sellers lose deals they should've won. The habits they've learned over time have left them inattentive to subtle nuances because they were on auto-pilot, acting without thinking. It's like a sign I heard about in the Alaskan wilderness, "Choose your rut. You'll be in it for the next 100 miles."

Wise sales leaders keep things fresh. They're always bringing new challenges to the table. They prevent their people from settling into a rut, always asking for a little bit more or to do something a little bit differently. This keeps them in the stretch zone and helps them continue to be their very best. With performance goals and process goals in place, and a specific plan for achieving them, you're ready to get started on the heart and soul of successful sales leadership— coaching.

Real Work Alert

The real work we'll be doing in the next two chapters builds on each other. It's a preparation worksheet for one-on-one meetings with your reps. In sales, we have pre-call planning sheets so salespeople don't show up unprepared for an appointment. This exercise is a pre-call planning sheet for your one-on-one's, so you're always prepared for these critically important meetings.

Here's step one in completing it. Write out the sales performance goal each sales rep who reports to you is accountable for delivering. You can do this by month, quarter, or year. Then identify the specific, repeated activities each rep needs to work on *right now* to move them closer to achieving his or her sales performance goal.

Salesperson:	
Sales Performance Goal	
Sales Process Goals Specific, repeated activities that move a person closer to achieving a sales performance goal	1.
	2.
	3.
	4.

A digital version of this worksheet is available online at www.billzipp.com/salessuccess.

One of the biggest mistakes I see sales leaders make related to setting goals with their salespeople is trying to do too much at one time, eating an elephant in a single bite. That's why the exercise above is limited to just four process goals.

While I'm fairly certain that the execution of your sales process requires more than doing four things well, no one, including you, can learn and master all those things at the same time. Less is more here. Identify the most critical process goals each salesperson who reports to you needs to work on right now and focus like a laser on them. This individual customization, and the adaptive coaching related to it which we address in the next chapter, will supercharge the performance of your salespeople and maximize the impact of your leadership.

Chapter Seven
COACHING

They have almost nothing in common with each other, the seasoned sales professional and the new sales hire. The experienced rep who's made President's Club for the last ten years and drives a beamer is as different as night from day with the twenty-something salesperson fresh out of college planning their first prospecting campaign.

Except for one thing.

And that one thing determines whether they'll be—or continue to be—successful in their job. What is it? Coaching.

It doesn't matter how well-traveled in sales you are, or how inexperienced, all of us need someone outside of ourselves giving input from that perspective. The best athletes have coaches, as well as the best actors and the best CEOs. And that's what successful sales managers do, they know how to coach their salespeople to be the very best. Do you?

A Simple Definition of Sales Coaching

Coaching has been all the rage the last few years. Google coaching and you'll get millions of responses and thousands of coaching models to follow. Ignore them all. Not because they're bad, but because they're unnecessarily complex and will not help you grow your salespeople.

Coaching salespeople, while not easy, has a simple two-part process to it (not an intricate ten-step model). These two parts are best captured in the sport of whitewater rafting. For years, I guided rafts down the whitewater rapids of the Deschutes River in Oregon. It was a demanding and exhilarating experience, holding the lives of eight screaming souls in your hands. Truly, some of the best weekends I've ever spent in my life have been on that river.

The key to success as a raft guide is being able to hit a rapid at its perfect center. If you do, the force of the rushing water will shoot you down the middle of the rapid, fast but safe. Miss the center, and you and your crew will be flipped out of the raft into a torrent of foam. Not fun (and sometimes quite dangerous).

So, you're always reading the river, staying in tune with what the water's doing, to hit the perfect center of each rapid. Hitting the perfect center, however, is not easy to do for one reason—rivers aren't straight. Rivers bend and twist and turn all over the place. As do their rapids. So, while you're reading the river, you also have to adjust your raft, pulling it to the left, pulling it to the right, or bringing it to a dead stop to keep from being dumped into the water.

This is an apt metaphor for the two-part process of successfully coaching salespeople. First, read the river. Pay close attention to the flow of your reps' development, for, like a river, it bends and twists and turns all over the place. Then adjust, adapting to these bends and twists and turns with the most effective coaching response. This is what it means to coach and coach well: read and respond, read and respond, read and respond.

Reading the river and responding accordingly perfectly parallels the principles of "Situational Leadership," a concept pioneered by Paul Hersey and Ken Blanchard in the business school classic, *Management of Organizational Behavior.*[12] I've adapted their principles here to the sales coaching environment. Situational sales leaders first assess the sales development of a rep before one word leaves their mouths, their responses being determined by the read of the river. Having assessed development, Situational Sales Coaching then selects the response that best matches the needs at hand. When this process is repeated over and over again, reps grow and sales soar because managers are providing the coaching the reps need when they need it.

Assessing Sales Development

How do you read the river? That is, how do you assess the sales development of your reps? There are two dynamics to determine development: competence and commitment. Competence is the proven, observable ability of a salesperson to complete a specific sales activity. Commitment is that salesperson's enthusiasm, motivation, or confidence related to that activity. One is external, the other is internal. One has to do with actions, and the other with attitude. A rep may be high or low in each dynamic, leading to four distinct development levels—low competence and high commitment, low competence and low commitment, high competence and low commitment, and high competence and high commitment.

When a salesperson is new to a particular sales activity, they often come to the task with a high degree of enthusiasm and motivation, eager to get going. The problem is, they don't know what they don't know and can make a mess of things, more than they could possibly imagine.

After a salesperson has been doing a particular sales activity for a while but hasn't mastered it yet, they can slide into a state of frustration and discouragement. They can't do the task very well and don't think they ever will, feeling overwhelmed and confused. Occasionally, however, they'll have flashes of competence. But these moments, like in my golf game, are rare.

If, however, salespeople persevere, they break through the competence barrier and begin to master a particular sales activity. The problem is, they're still not sure of themselves because mastery is so new to them. They have competence but very little confidence in their competence. As a result, they're capable but cautious, productive but tentative.

Finally, when salespeople have mastered a particular sales activity and have all the enthusiasm and motivation in the world to do it, they're consistently competent and supremely confident. They're inspired and inspire others, able to be given a high degree of independence in the task. The problem at this level of development is this: without an ongoing challenge, these salespeople can get bored and make dumb mistakes (or go work for another company).

Development Level 1	Development Level 2	Development Level 3	Development Level 4
LOW Competence and HIGH Commitment	LOW Competence and LOW Commitment	HIGH Competence and LOW Commitment	HIGH Competence and HIGH Commitment
Descriptors:	**Descriptors:**	**Descriptors:**	**Descriptors:**
Inexperienced Eager Enthusiastic Optimistic *Don't know what they don't know*	Frustrated Discouraged Overwhelmed Confused *Yet with flashes of competence*	Capable but Cautious Productive but Tentative *No confidence in his or her competence*	Consistent Inspired Inspires Others Independent *Yet if not challenged, will get bored*

Another way of looking at these four stages of development is this. The first stage is *unconscious incompetence.* That is, this person doesn't know what they don't know. The next stage in development is *conscious incompetence,* a person knows—all too painfully well—what they don't know. Then a breakthrough occurs, and competence grows. But it's cautious and tentative, *conscious competence.* Finally, full mastery emerges, and high performance is achieved almost without thinking. This is the fourth stage of development: *unconscious competence.*

Matching Sales Coaching Style

Each bend and twist and turn in the river of sales development has a matching response. As reading the river, a situational sales coach responds adaptively to the flow that presents itself. That is, they match their coaching style to the needs of the development level that exists within each rep related to a particular sales activity. Like development, sales coaching styles have two dynamics as well—direction and support.

Direction involves teaching, training, planning, correcting, and providing accountability. Support involves asking, listening, reflecting, encouraging, and providing autonomy. Various combinations of being high or low in providing direction and support define the matching coaching style each development level needs.

For a salesperson at Development Level 1 at a particular sales activity, low competence and high commitment, the matching coaching style is high direction and low support. As you work with this sales rep, affirm their enthusiasm and define success very clearly. Teach and show them how to do this task by providing concrete examples and checking for understanding along the way. This is Sales Coaching Style 1.

With a salesperson at Development Level 2 at a particular sales activity, low competence and high commitment, you have no margin for error. They don't know how to complete the particular sales activity and they really don't want to either. So you must respond with high direction and high support. You do this by understanding their frustrations and letting them vent their emotions. Analyze their failures in a safe, nonjudgmental environment, and help them learn from each, filling in training gaps. This is the time to explain why a certain task needs to be done in a certain way, and while you're doing that, take the time to provide perspective when those flashes of competence occur. They are actually making progress, even though it doesn't feel like it. This is Sales Coaching Style 2.

Sales Coaching Style 3 takes a very different tack. A salesperson at Development Level 3 related to a particular sales activity does not have confidence in their own competence, so less is more in coaching them. Using low direction and high support, ask lots of questions and listen, reflecting back what you hear them saying. Your objective is to help this rep his own voice, find his own way, and become self-sufficient. A perfect adaptive response to most of their inquiries is, "How did you solve a problem like that the last time you faced it?" or, more briefly, "What would you do?" This is called appreciative inquiry, classic Style 3 Coaching, and will help your reps analyze their successes, and again, hear their own voices.

Sales Coaching Style 4 is the perfect adaptive match for Development Level 4. The capable, confident salesperson in a particular task needs a leader that treats him or her more like a partner and a peer than a subordinate with low direction and low support. Let her talk about her favorite subject (herself), celebrate her successes, and recognize her publicly. Provide autonomy around this particular sales activity, using her expertise in it to help you teach others, and push for a little bit more to keep them from getting bored.

Sales Coaching Style 1	Sales Coaching Style 2	Sales Coaching Style 3	Sales Coaching Style 4
HIGH Direction and LOW Support	HIGH Direction and HIGH Support	LOW Direction and HIGH Support	LOW Direction and LOW Support
Behaviors:	**Behaviors:**	**Behaviors:**	**Behaviors:**
Affirm enthusiasm Define success clearly Give concrete examples Teach and show HOW Check for understanding *Check work frequently*	Understand frustrations Analyze failures Provide perspective Explain WHY Fill in learning gaps *Check work consistently*	Ask questions and listen Analyze successes Provide reassurance Help hear own voice Clear path of problems *Check work regularly*	Treat as a partner/peer Celebrate successes Provide autonomy Use to teach others Push for a little bit more *Check work occasionally*

Another way of looking at these four coaching styles is this. Sales Coaching Style One involves you, or someone else on your team, completing a specific sales activity while a salesperson watches it being done so he or she learns what good looks like. This may involve shadowing a seasoned seller on a call or listening in to an executive overview. Sales Coaching Style Two is more participatory, as you (or someone else) completes part of a sales activity and the salesperson learning how to master it completes the other part, like a pilot with co-pilot learning how to fly an airplane.

Sales Coaching Style Three involves you (or, again, someone else on your team) observing another salesperson completing a specific sales activity and then discussing how it went. This is Style One in reverse, with plenty of open-ended questions on your part so this salesperson hears their own voice and finds their own way in mastering a particular sales activity. In short, this involves shadowing a rep and having a conversation afterwards. Finally, as you apply each of these coaching styles, Sales Coaching Style Four releases a salesperson to act on their own related to the activity at hand.

These four are summarized in twelve simple words: I do, you watch. We do. You do, I watch. You do.

Please note that all coaching styles provide accountability for the completion of a task. That is, they always check a salesperson's work. Each style, however, provides it differently at differing time intervals.

Sales Coaching Style 1, when a rep is new to a particular task, checks-in frequently, at least once a day, to see how things are going. When a person is first acquiring a skill, they need near-instant feedback to learn it quickly. These check-ins don't need to be, and most definitely should *not* be, long, drawn-out meetings. Just five to ten minutes here and five to ten minutes there will do the trick.

When a salesperson is muddling through Development Level 2, they're still learning a particular task, but they also have frustrations related to it. I don't think you need as frequent check-ins in this stage as with Development Level 1, but you should still provide consistent follow-through. I check-in using this coaching style with every other day meetings, fifteen to thirty minutes long, which allow for the venting of emotion to blow off some steam and focused equipping to build sales competence.

Development Level 3 and Development Level 4 also need accountability but with a lighter touch. Time frequencies that work in these stages vary between once a week to once a month, but make sure you still check-in. The tendency in sales leadership is to let the squeaky wheel get the grease, ignoring your top performers. Nature being what it is, proceeding from order to disorder, soon your top performers won't be your top performers anymore.

Check-ins, though, look very different in Sales Coaching Styles 3 and 4 than in Sales Coaching Styles 1 and 2. In fact, they don't feel like check-ins at all, but they still provide accountability. The key in these styles is getting the rep to talk about everything that's going on in his or her business and encouraging communication by saying, "Tell me more … Tell me more…" When you do this well, everything you need to know as a sales manager will be told to you without the rep even realizing they've done so. Brilliant!

Development Level 1	Development	Development	Development
LOW Competence and HIGH Commitment	LOW Competence and LOW Commitment	HIGH Competence and LOW Commitment	HIGH Competence and HIGH Commitment
↑↓	↑↓	↑↓	↑↓
Sales Coaching Style 1	Sales Coaching Style 2	Sales Coaching Style 3	Sales Coaching Style 4
HIGH Direction and LOW Support	HIGH Direction and HIGH Support	LOW Direction and HIGH Support	LOW Direction and LOW Support

How Read and Respond Works in Real Life

Here's how this process looks in the real world of working with your salespeople. Imagine having a new sales hire whom you are trying to teach how to use your company's sales CRM system. You wouldn't give them their user name and password and let them play around with the software and get back to you in a few weeks. That would be foolish!

Coaching that's true to Style 1 thanks this rep for their enthusiasm in learning the CRM system, and then very clearly and very specifically walks the rep through it step by step. It shows this person how to enter data into the system in the very best way, and how to pull reports from the data as well. It asks the new hire to shadow a more seasoned rep who's a whiz at it and touches base with them at the end of each day to see how he or she is coming along. You might even have a sales CRM certification class they can take, successfully completing the class in the first few weeks on the job.

As I'm sure you know, however, adoption rates by sales reps of CRM systems are abysmally low, so it's entirely possible for you to do all the things I outlined in the paragraph above and this rep may still not master the software. In fact, it's not just possible but probable. One day they blurt out after another failed attempt to pull a report from the system, "How can I make any sales when all I do is spend my time in front of a stupid computer? I could just smash this thing to pieces!"

What's your best response here? To listen, empathize, and counterintuitively, let them vent even more. Then lean in and continue training and equipping. No one gets anything the first time through, and most everyone goes through a detour of disillusionment in the learning process. This is also the time to explain why it's so important to get customer data into the system and make the connection between accurate information and robust sales. Collect success stories on this topic and tell them one by one.

Now imagine a sales rep who used to put all his data in the CRM system perfectly like clockwork, but over the last few months, hasn't even logged into the app. You ask him in your one-on-one what's going on, and he tells you that he doesn't find the software that helpful anymore and has basically given up on it. Your temptation here is to use a variation of Coaching Style 1 to deal with this problem by telling him, "Just do it!"

This will backfire, however, because when a person knows how to do something but is not to doing it, they don't need more information (direction) but more inspiration (support). Interactions with him should involve questions that help him hear his own voice and find his own way. Here's a list of questions I've used to address this challenge:

- Remember the prospect list you pulled at the beginning of the first quarter? If I recall, over 50% of them ended up doing business with us. How did having the right data help you there?
- Have you ever forgot anything in your life? How can completely capturing customer information act as an extension of your brain?
- When you used the CRM system on a regular basis, was there a particular time of the day or day of the week that you did it? Did you block out that time or just do it whenever you felt like it? How were you successful at doing it once? How can we duplicate that success?
- I know you want to be a sales manager one day. How might *not* doing this task affect your brand in the company and impact future leadership plans?

Notice how all these questions put the ball back into this salesperson's court. "Just do it!" as tempting as it may be, is extremely ineffective in Development Level 3 and should be used as a last resort (if at all). The best response is to draw a person like this out, asking questions and eliciting answers until they self-correct and own the task for themselves.

The final sales coaching temptation comes from ignoring the rep who perfectly uses the CRM system every week without fail. As I said earlier, human nature being what it is, when you do that, this person is likely to slide from order to disorder, becoming the Development Level 3 example I just referred to. The key here is having her tell you every month the wonderful things she's doing with the CRM system. Another Sales Coaching Style 4 activity is using her for your success stories, both publicly and privately. Then deputizing her as the CRM expert on the team, becoming the go-to person, instead of you, for all teaching and training on it. This will keep her from getting bored with the task and drifting.

All Assessment is Task Specific

Finally, I'd like you to observe how many times I used the words "a particular sales activity" in the paragraphs above (by my count, sixteen times). There's a reason for that repetition. All assessment of sales development is task specific. Development Levels 1, 2, 3, and 4 are not generic categories into which we sort individual salespeople, like students at Hogwarts's School of Witchcraft and Wizardry. They're dynamic descriptions, all four of which could be true for the same exact salesperson at the same exact time.

You may have a rep who is new to the task of writing clear, concise, and compelling prospecting email and be at Development Level 1 in that task. The same rep could be super frustrated with your company's sales CRM system and ready to smash his laptop to pieces. That's Development Level 2, as explained above. Yet when it comes to this rep's closing deals, he's quite capable, but lacks confidence, because he once lost a huge deal in closing and is still a little unsure of himself. In this task, he's at Development Level 3. Then, when it comes to presenting an executive overview in a first appointment, he's amazing. You use the recordings of his calls as an example for everyone else on your team and hold him up as your executive overview expert. This, of course, is Development Level 4.

See how the same sales rep can be at different development levels all at the same time, depending on the specific activity that needs to be completed? The key to coaching is first defining the task at hand, or what I outlined in Chapter 6 on clarifying sales process goals. Based on these goals, you then determine each rep's competence and commitment related to them, and finally, adapt your coaching style to the needs of that development level, using the perfect blend of direction and support. Here's an exercise to help you do that.

Real Work Alert

For the real work we'll be doing in this chapter, return to the One-on-One Meeting Planner we started working on in Chapter 6. In that exercise you identified three to four sales process goals you want each of your reps to master right now. It's time to assess their development, that is their competence and commitment, related to each of these goals.

Salesperson:		
Sales Performance Goal		
Sales Process Goals Specific, repeated activities that move a person closer to achieving a sales performance goal	1.	
	Competence ☐ Low to Some ☐ Mostly High	Commitment ☐ Low to Variable ☐ Mostly High
	Circle Development Level: 1 2 3 4	
	2.	
	Competence ☐ Low to Some ☐ Mostly High	Commitment ☐ Low to Variable ☐ Mostly High
	Circle Development Level: 1 2 3 4	

3.	

Competence	Commitment
☐ Low to Some	☐ Low to Variable
☐ Mostly High	☐ Mostly High

Circle Development Level: 1   2   3   4

4.	

Competence	Commitment
☐ Low to Some	☐ Low to Variable
☐ Mostly High	☐ Mostly High

Circle Development Level: 1   2   3   4

A digital version of this worksheet is available online at
www.billzipp.com/salessuccess.

You've now completed the first step of effective sales coaching. You've read the river. That is, you've completed an assessment of the sales development for each of your salespeople related to the specific process goals they are working on right now. When the sales leaders I train finish this exercise, lightning strikes. They see for the very first time in black and white that the salespeople who report to them are at dramatically different stages of development related to the critical activities they are being asked to do. Yes, that's it!

Now it's time to take the second step of effective sales coaching—responding accordingly. Based on the assessment of your sales reps' development, what adaptive sales coaching strategies are you going to take as you interreact with them about their process goals? How are you going to give them the coaching they need when they need it? Complete this exercise, and you're ready to rock your one-on-one's.

Salesperson:	
Development Level for Process Goal One:	
Sales coaching strategies for Process Goal One	
Development Level for Process Goal Two:	
Sales coaching strategies for Process Goal Two	

Development Level for Process Goal Three:	
Sales coaching strategiesfor Process Goal Three	
Development Level for Process Goal Four:	
Sales coaching strategies for Process Goal Four	

A digital version of this worksheet is available online at www.billzipp.com/salessuccess.

Chapter Eight

ONE-ON-ONES

Before we dive into the single most important thing you can do to develop your salespeople—conducting consistent, effective one-on-ones with them—it makes sense to look back at where we've been in this section on mobilization. Our discussions on mobilization so far can be summarized in two pairs of sales leadership practices: setting performance goals and setting process goals, reading the river and responding accordingly.

In the sales context, goal setting has two key components. There's revenue generation by month, quarter, and year, or what I call performance goals. These targets are important—try running a sales department without them; it's a nightmare—but they're not enough, because they don't specify exactly how they are to be achieved. So in setting goals with your salespeople, it's necessary to add another layer of focus: process goals.

Process goals are the specific sales activities that need to be repeated every day, week, or month to actually achieve one's performance goals. Performance goals are a salesperson's target marathon time for the fiscal year, so to speak, and process goals are that person's weekly running workouts. Pair one done.

The second pair of sales leadership practices we've been discussing builds on the first. When coaching your salespeople, it's important to assess their development before opening your mouth and offering any kind of advice, much like a doctor would diagnose a patient before writing a prescription (I don't press the doctor/patient analogy too much, however, because your salespeople aren't sick and you aren't the cure).

You conduct this assessment by understanding a rep's competence and commitment related to completing a sales process goal and then adapting your response to the needs of his or her development. Your sales coaching may be more directive in one case, more supportive in another, or a dynamic mix of both. The coaching response you choose to use with your salespeople is determined by the level of their development related to a specific sales process goal (not experience or seniority).

The metaphor we've been using to illustrate this dynamic is rafting down the rapids of a river. Each whitewater rapid you encounter is different, twisting and turning to the right or to the left, so you're always reading the river. That is, accurately assessing the situation before you. Then you respond accordingly, steering your raft with the rapid so you shoot down the center of its vortex. Fast but safe.

Now both of these pairs come together in one powerful practice: conducting regular one-on-ones with your salespeople. The problem is, no one tells you how to have these meetings. They just insist that you do. Worse yet, no one else really wants to have them either. A head of sales I worked with once said, "There are two kinds of people in a sales organization who hate having one-on-ones. Sales managers and sales representatives." Guess what? That's everybody!

If you're the head of sales, this is bad news. When people hate the single most important thing they can do to develop your sales reps, they'll use any excuse to avoid it or do the bare minimum to check it off their lists. If you're a sales manager, this is bad news too. In your gut, you know you should have regular one-on-ones, not to get your manager off your back but because they'll make a really big difference in the success of your team. You just don't know how.

Over the last twenty years of sales leadership, I've conducted thousands of one-on-ones with salespeople and sales managers alike. As a consultant, I've sat in on other leaders' one-on-ones and debriefed the meetings with them afterward. Over this time, I've developed a proven process to complete this critical practice. Here are the five essential steps for an effective sales one-on-one:

STEP ONE: The Agenda

Regular one-on-one meetings between a sales representative and his or her sales manager should focus on one thing and one thing only: goals. This meeting is not a time for deal reviews, which are best done with the entire team so everyone can learn from the review, pipeline management, forecasting, or strategic account development—all best done with the entire team as well (or the occasional one-off). Neither is this a time for corrective action. When corrective action needs to take place, as it sometimes does, it should be done outside of the regular one-on-one, so a sales rep knows what to expect whenever they meet with you. No surprises!

Goals, that's the agenda of an effective sales on-on-one. Don't be fooled, however, by the simplicity of that statement, because as we've discussed (perhaps *ad nauseam* for you), there are two distinct kinds of goals to focus on with your salespeople, performance goals and process goals, and the latter set the agenda for all your one-on-ones. Not just generic process goals, however. The genius of this personalized meeting is it allows you to get very specific with an individual sales rep and focus on his or her unique development needs.

For example, conducting five executive overviews per week that lead to at least two submitted proposals may be one of your company's sales process goals. But when you sat in with a rep during a couple of his executive overviews last week, you observed that he's doing most of the talking, asking very few questions and sucking the oxygen out of the call. No wonder, you say to yourself, so few of his executive overviews move forward in the pipeline.

Here's an opportunity in your next one-on-one with this rep to provide customized coaching, directing him to ask more questions in his executive overviews, to wait for the answers, and listen—really listen— to a prospective customer. Together you define exactly what that means for a thirty-minute sales call, and you follow up by sitting in on a few more of his executive overviews. This is like my running coach observing my gait during our weekly workouts and giving me feedback to improve the length of my stride and the strike of my feet on the ground. I still complete my weekly running workouts, but with her coaching, I do it with greater effectiveness and improved results.

The agenda, then, for all the one-on-ones you have with all of your salespeople is a handful of very specific sales development goals each rep is working on to improve his or her execution of your company's sales process. Imagine the impact of getting input like this every week of every year, rather than the empty cheerleading, "Just sell, baby!" that most sales managers manufacture.

STEP TWO: The Flow

Once you've set individualized sales process goals, the good news about having regular sales one-on-ones is this: they follow a simple structure—banks on the river, so to speak—that allow the meeting to flow from one phase to the next. The outline for this flow is easy to remember and easy to follow.

First, talk about **progress**. Progress on what? Progress on a rep's individualized process goals. (Are you sick of this concept yet? I bet you are! Sorry, but it's central to successful sales leadership.) The focus in this part of the meeting is on past performance and sets the trajectory for the rest of the meeting. If you're having a sales one-on-one like this for the very first time, work together on defining a rep's process goals, then in every meeting after this one, start by checking in on progress related to them.

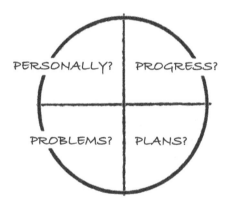

Then talk about **plans**. The focus in this part of the meeting is not on the past but on the future. That is, given the progress this person has achieved related to their process goals, what are they going to do in the next few weeks to maintain that progress or even expand on it? Don't let this part of the conversation become broad and generic. Drill down to identify tangible, measurable steps of action to take in the immediate future to continue to make developmental improvements. Next, the meeting shifts to the present, as in right now what **problems** are getting in their way and how are they doing **personally**? Find out what you can do to remove any obstacles that may be exist in your team members' sales world and listen intently to what's going on in their personal world.

A slight variation of this order occurs when you have a salesperson who's highly relational. He or she may not be able to adequately discuss past **progress** or future **plans** until they've told you how they're doing **personally**. If that's the case—and in my experience about a third of the time it is—I start with how they're doing **personally** and then move to **progress**, **plans**, and **problems**. I give this counsel with a warning, however. If you, too, are highly relational, and you start with how your people are doing personally, it's entirely possible to burn up fifteen minutes or more talking about last week's soccer match or an upcoming birthday party. That's not the point of this portion of the meeting. It's simply to stay checked-in with each other's life. If more time is needed, go to the pub after work. Finally, I never start with **problems**, although I always reserve time to talk about them. It just sets thing off in a negative direction.

How long should a meeting like this go? Forty-five minutes. That's it. I've followed this flow thousands of times and find with a regular weekly one-on-one (See: STEP FOUR below), I can wrap things up at about a quarter till the hour, capture salient points in my journal, stand up, go for a short walk, and be ready for the next meeting at the top of the hour.

STEP THREE: The Conversation

It's important to understand, as you work through the flow of a one-on-one from the past to the future and the present, that this meeting is a conversation, and a conversation involves both parties speaking and listening. The biggest mistake I made as a new sales manager was dominating the discussion in my one-on-ones. I observe this same mistake being made whenever I sit in on one-on-ones during a sales consulting project. Here's a typical post-meeting debrief:

"How do you think that one-on-one went?"

"Okay, I guess," a sales manager says.

"Who did most of the talking?" I ask.

"Oh … I did."

"How much? 80%? 90%? 100?" I probe.

"Not 100%," he or she laughs uncomfortably. "Probably 80–90%."

"So, if you're doing 80–90% of the talking in your one-on-ones, how much do you think your salespeople are getting out of them?"

"Not much," is the honest reply.

The answer, however, to this problem is not its opposite, letting a sales rep do 80–90% of the talking in your one-one-ones. The answer is returning to the principles of sales coaching in Chapter Seven and letting the template presented there shape your conversations. If a salesperson is at Development Level 4 related to a particular sales activity, they should, in fact, do most of the talking related to it. You may interject occasionally, mostly to affirm what this person is saying and to nudge him or her forward in their growth, but this is the coaching style that allows a rep to chat about their favorite subject (themselves). If, conversely, a salesperson is at Development Level 1 related to a particular sales activity, you do most of the talking. Not all of the talking, but most of it, taking regular breaks to check for understanding and affirm their enthusiasm.

Coaching Style 2 and Coaching Style 3 are both two-directional and where you're likely to spend most of your time as a sales leader. Both styles ask lots of questions and listen to the responses being given, but the difference between them is what you do after receiving your answers. Coaching Style 3, because it's convinced that this person knows how to complete the sales activity under consideration, stays in question-asking mode, always putting the ball back into the other person's court. The reason for this tactic is to help reps hear their own voice and find their own way. Less is more in this style. If you answer questions for your salespeople that they already know the answers to, all you'll do is create a codependent relationship from which they'll never emerge to be a fully functioning sales professional.

Coaching Style 2, however, after receiving answers to its questions, takes an additional step by leaning in and giving direction. To be sure, this style includes elements of a rep's response in that direction (much like you would use a prospect's own words in writing a customized proposal for them), but when a salesperson is still in the learning mode related to a particular process goal, gaps remain in their development, and it's your responsibility to fill in those gaps. Sometimes in a one-on-one, you won't know whether to use Coaching Style 2 or Coaching Style 3 until you hear the answers to the questions you pose, but that's the beauty of this template: you can pivot from one coaching style to the another quite easily, either by leaning in and giving direction or backing off and staying in question-asking mode.

Finally, I'd like to remind you that critical to any good conversation is being fully present in it. Under no circumstances should you allow email, texts, phone calls, or anything else distract you during this time. Silence your phone and turn off all notifications on your laptop. If you're conducting a one-on-one remotely, always have the video camera on in *both* locations. Multitasking is okay if you're watching a football game and folding the laundry. It doesn't matter if you mismatch your socks or miss an interception. It does matter when you miss a subtle emotional cue from a sales rep who's struggling because you were reading an incoming text.

STEP FOUR: The Cadence

After the question, "What should I do in a sales one-on-one?" the most frequent question I get is, "How often should I have them?" I won't answer that question like a typical consultant, as in, "It depends."

Over the years, I've learned that the best cadence for sales one-on-ones is once a week. Here's why I believe that.

Most everything in sales has a thirty- to sixty-day echo effect. If you uncover a problem and resolve it, that resolution won't impact sales results for another thirty to sixty days. Meeting once a month is too infrequent not to have that math work against you, especially if a meeting gets missed for some reason. This echo effect is why I don't recommend every other week one-on-ones either. Every-other-week meetings can inadvertently slip into a once-a-month meeting with a sick day, vacation day, or a scheduling conflict, and you'll find yourself, again, losing a month—if not a whole quarter. Many a quota has been missed due to one bad sales month.

For more seasoned sellers, if we've made all our one-on-ones, I'll cancel the last meeting of the month and let them focus on closing deals, conducting three meetings with them in a month rather than four. For less seasoned sellers, I'll use that extra time to double up on meetings for a week or so, giving them extra attention.

View these times in your week as you would a doctor's appointment. If you had a doctor's appointment on Friday, how would you—in your crazy-busy week—make sure you got there? You'd put it in your calendar, of course, and not let anything take its place. Treat your sales one-on-ones in the same way. They're the most important thing you do as a sales leader and deserve to be scheduled in this protected, dare I say sacred, way.

Finally, I used to do all my one-on-ones in one day, but then I'd get to the end of the day utterly exhausted with a splitting headache. So, I blocked out a morning in one part of the week and an afternoon in the other part of the week to do three or four in each block. Using the forty-five minutes on and fifteen minutes off pattern I recommended earlier, I began to look forward to these days instead of dreading them. You will too.

STEP FIVE: The Follow-Through

I hate running on a treadmill. I've tried it, and it doesn't work for me. Mostly because it's so unfulfilling. No matter the fancy screen or the dramatic video that's playing, I always feel like I'm going nowhere. Give me point A to point B any time, even with our cold Northwest winter rain. Apart from consistent follow-through, this is exactly what a sales one-on-one feels like: a treadmill going nowhere, recycling the same issues over and over again and repeating the same talk tracks. No growth, no progress, no change.

The final step in having effective one-on-ones is keeping track of your commitments in them, and that means one thing: taking good notes. We use CRM software in sales because we can't remember the details of the deals we have in the pipeline. The same is true for one-on-ones. Taking notes is a way of capturing both parties' commitments so you can remember them, and most importantly, do them.

Ask your sales reps to take notes during the first half of the one-on-one on progress and plans. That is, have them summarize your discussions related to past development on their goals and the specific steps of action that comprise their future plans. Then ask them to send these notes to you. They can do this by taking a picture of the things they've written down during the meeting or send you a copy of what they wrote down afterward via email. Either way, you get to see if their understanding of the conversation is aligned with your understanding of the conversation, and their sending it to you reinforces accountability.

You may also take notes of the first half of a one-on-one, but what you should really keep track of is the second half: problems that are getting in the way, what both of you can do you to remove them, and how this person is doing personally. These comprise the critically important information for successful sales leadership.

I prefer to take notes in these meetings with pen and paper in a journal, which allows me to maintain eye contact and keeps me from digital distractions on my computer. That may not be your cup of tea but just have a system that works for you *without fail.* There's nothing more discouraging than pouring out your heart to your sales manager and the next week having to do it all over again because he totally forgot what you said. Don't be that manager!

When it's time to have another one-on-one, just pull out these notes and start there. The last meeting's plans become this meeting's progress, and updates are given on present problems and personal developments. Simple.

The Bottom Line on One-on-One's

Here's my bottom line on this. As I've said repeatedly in this chapter, having consistent, effective one-on-ones with your reps is the single-most important thing you can do to develop your salespeople. It's the difference between consistently hitting goal and missing it every other month (or more). It's the difference between building a team of strong, capable professionals, and the revolving door of sales personnel most companies struggle with.

My challenge to you is to become a sales one-on-one expert. Focus sharply on its agenda, learn its flow, master its communication, keep its cadence, and maintain consistent follow-through. Doing so will yield the rich reward of above goal performance year after year and team members who'll be completely loyal to your leadership.

In the next chapter we're going to look at the other kinds of meetings you need to conduct as a sales leader—the weekly, quarterly and yearly team meetings—and how to be effective in them as well.

Chapter Nine

TEAM MEETINGS

Let me be brutally honest with you. Sales team meetings are a set up for disaster. There, I've said it. Here's why.

First, salespeople are action-oriented. They don't like sitting in meetings. It's not in their DNA. For most of your sellers, school was a painful experience for this very reason, and your sales meetings remind them of being in school. Salespeople are kinesthetic. They like being active, out and about. That's why they're in sales. Most certainly, they don't like being stuck in a room, no matter how fancy that room may be.

Second, salespeople receive compensation from being engaged in sales activity, not from sitting in meetings. Every minute in a meeting is a minute that keeps them from making money. "Is this meeting worth it?" That's the question always on their minds, sometimes with an invisible calculator adding up opportunities lost. Sadly, most of the meetings they attend aren't worth it. Not even close.

Finally, sales meetings are a set up for disaster because your salespeople have endured so many bad meetings. Five years ago, I had some pre-cancerous cells burned off the side of my face. My dermatologist assured me it was no big deal. Just a pin prick or two and everything would be alright. Wow, was he wrong. I walked out of the clinic feeling as though I'd been slapped in the face a thousand times over. This is the history most salespeople bring into a meeting, however well-intentioned you may be. They've attended plenty of sales meetings. Their manager assured them they were no big deal. That manager was wrong. Everyone walked out feeling like they'd been slapped in the face a thousand times over.

The great irony about sales meetings is this: they have the amazing potential to transform your team. When done correctly, they can light the fire of passion within your sellers' souls and fan that flame into a raging fire. When done well, they can establish a winning sales culture and deepen everyone's commitment to it. And when done right, they can put into the hands of your salespeople the resources they need to make more money, a lot more money.

Here's how to make team meetings matter again, or perhaps, matter for the very first time.

A Template for Every Meeting

Sales meetings that matter don't happen by accident. They take planning and persistence. But with the right planning, you can bring overwhelming value to every meeting. Then, by persisting in providing this value, you'll win over your salespeople and get to a place where they actually enjoy attending your meetings. Believe me, that's possible. I've seen it with my own eyes.

Well-planned sales meetings have four key elements to them: inspiration, instruction, interaction, and information. Use these four as a template to prepare for all your meetings.

1. Inspiration

Selling is hard work. If it wasn't, everyone would be a successful salesperson. Everyone most certainly is not a successful salesperson. Sales is like riding a bicycle uphill with the wind in your face, all day, every day. The crazy thing is, most of the salespeople I know are fine with that. They love the challenge of the climb and wouldn't want to live their lives any other way.

Here's what they don't want. They don't want the captain of their cycling team adding to that challenge. While they're working hard riding uphill with the wind in their face, they don't want their manager cruising in a car next to them criticizing their form for the whole world to hear. In fact, they want just the opposite: words of encouragement that get them to the front of the pack.

The leadership adage, praise in public and correct in private, applies here in spades. Rarely is public correction in a sales meeting effective. That kind of slap in the face is humiliating and demotivating. Just the opposite, however, is energizing and inspiring: public recognition and reward. Tell the story of a recent sales success with a rep in the room as the hero of that story. Give out gift cards to everyone who's completed a certain number of outbound calls that resulted in a new appointment and cheer for each person as he or she comes to the front of the room to get his or her card. Celebrate birthdays, work anniversaries, new logos, won deals, whatever. Begin every meeting by amping up the emotional tone with the power of positive praise. (Re-read Chapter Four for more ideas.)

Again, this stuff doesn't happen by accident. You can't show up to a meeting and off the top of your head deliver meaningful recognition and reward. Inspirational team meetings take time and planning, but the effort is worth it. More that worth it!

2. Instruction

Not only is selling hard work, it's complicated work as well. Like golf, there's always something new to learn, always something else to work on. The minute you think driving off the tee is going well, you've got to work on your short game. The round where your fairway irons hit every green is the same round where you three-putt ten times. There's always something!

I hate golf, but I love sales because of the life-long learning opportunities it provides. Embrace this dynamic in all your sales team meetings. From a ten-minute tip to all day training, teach your sellers how to sell even better than they do already.

Just make sure to vet any instruction you provide. All sales are not the same. If your product or service has one decision maker and requires one call to close, find training that teaches your sellers how to quickly connect with prospects and direct discussions to a done deal. If, however, your product or service has a committee of decision makers and takes eighteen months to close, the training you provide should teach something totally different.

Yes, all sales are not the same, and all sales training is not the same either. Just because someone has the word "sales" in the title of a book, it doesn't mean it's valid training at all. Be on the lookout for the content that speaks specifically to your needs, then use all the materials—books, exercises, online courses, and YouTube videos—with your team. Again this takes time and planning, but nothing will move the number more than providing your salespeople with exactly the right resources they need to succeed.

3. Interaction

Return to the beginning of this chapter and re-read the second paragraph. See that word "kinesthetic"? Kinesthetic refers to a learning style that learns by doing. Auditory learners learn by hearing, but most adults—and most salespeople for that matter—aren't auditory learners. They're kinesthetic learners. Yet we persist in stuffing them into a room and talking to them, on and on and on and on and on.

The third part of your sales meeting template addresses this dynamic. Salespeople will master the concepts you're sharing with them when they're presented in an environment that allows them to fully participate in the process. That means setting aside one-way communication, or keeping it to a bare minimum, and using discussion groups, games, contests, role plays, and learning exercises. This isn't fluff, and don't let anyone tell you that it is. It's wise recognition that kinesthetic learners need active engagement to understand and apply any content that's being presented to them.

Interaction also involves using other people on your sales team to provide instruction in a meeting. This brilliantly accomplishes four things all at the same time. It, of course, takes the pressure off you to do everything in a meeting. It also allows an individual salesperson to master the topic at hand, for whenever we teach something, we're forced to learn it in a deeper way. It also creates peer-to-peer interactions, which increase the quality of teamwork, and quite pragmatically, it lets other team members experience firsthand how challenging it is to keep the attention of a bunch of driven kinesthetic learners. Maybe, just maybe, they'll pay better attention when you're leading the next meeting.

There's another important reason to conduct interactive team meetings. Your salespeople are on the frontline of the marketplace. They're seeing things no one else in your company is seeing, and they're experiencing things no one else in your company is experiencing.

Interaction takes the time to talk with them about the pulse of the marketplace.

Trust your salespeople with questions that are difficult and, perhaps, even a little bit awkward. And listen. Really listen. What you'll receive in return is increased engagement, deepened ownership, and priceless market intelligence. It was a salesperson who alerted Intel in 1979 that Motorola had developed a faster, easier to program microprocessor and was killing them in the marketplace. Intel's President and Chief Operating Officer, the legendary Andy Grove, listened to that salesperson, and the rest is history.[13]

4. Information

Okay, now it's time for you to talk. Sharing information is last in the team meeting template not because it's the least important, but because inspiration, instruction, and interaction set the table for it. When you, in the words of Steven Covey, "seek first to understand, then to be understood,"[14] you'll find the things that usually get ignored are more positively received by your team.

This is the time to communicate corporate developments and coordinate the company calendar. This is also the time to share information on progress toward goal, product changes, and pricing details. If you work in a larger organization, there will be immense pressure to make this the most extensive part of your meeting. The reality of corporate life is that information expands to fill the time given it (and then some). Resist this pressure to make your team meetings a dumping ground for cooperate dictums. Review stuff at a high level, follow-up with email, and use technology, like HighSpot or Slack, to do the heavy lifting for you.

Nevertheless, it's super important for your team to have access to current, relevant information. Even with our children out of the house, I'm still surprised by how easy it is for my wife and I not to be in synch regarding upcoming dates and details. So once a week we sit down over coffee and coordinate our calendars. If there's two or more people on your sales team, you need to do the same. Anyone who's worked with me has heard me say these words, "Over-communicate by a factor of ten." There's usually a comedian or two in the meeting who does an impression of me saying this. I love it when they do, because it proves to me they've got the point. Over-communicate by a factor of ten.

Real Work Alert

This is a simple exercise, but one that will transform your sales meetings. Take a piece of paper, or open a document on your laptop, and write out these four words: Inspiration, Instruction, Interaction, and Information. Now make a list of items under each heading that answer the following questions:

Inspiration

- Who's achieved something significant in the last few weeks? New appointments set? New logos won? New skills acquired? New deals done? How can you acknowledge this in a meaningful way at an upcoming meeting?
- Who's reached a significant milestone in the last few weeks? Consecutive months over goal? An extraordinarily large deal? The completion of a special project? How can you acknowledge this in a meaningful way at an upcoming meeting?
- Who's had something positive happen in their personal life in the last few weeks? A birthday, an anniversary, the birth of a baby, a new house, a new car, a graduation? How can you celebrate this together as a team?

Instruction

- What's a critical sales skill that most everyone needs refreshed on? What article, video, case study, or role-play can you use to sharpen your team's ability related to this skill?
- What's a new sales skill your team needs to master due to a shift in the marketplace? What article, video, case study, or role-play can you use to sharpen everyone's ability related to this skill?
- What non-sales skill, like time management, cross-functional communication, or financial acumen, does your team need to master? What content will you use to help develop these skills in their life?

Interaction

- What two-way communication strategies can you employ in providing the instruction above? Discussion groups? Learning exercises? Town hall open forums?
- Are there difficult but important questions about what's going on in the marketplace, which need to be discussed openly and honestly as a team? The quality of your product and/or service? The terms for your product and/or service? A new competitor? The economy?
- Who other than you—both inside and outside your team—can be deputized to help provide inspiration, instruction, interaction, and information in your meetings? What senior leaders can you invite to your meetings so the members of your team begin to build executive sponsorship within the organization?

Information

- Where is individual and team progress toward goal for the current month, quarter, and year?

- What new product, product development, and/or pricing details need to be communicated to the team?
- What upcoming dates on the company's calendar need to be kept top of mind?
- What helpful personnel policies need to be reviewed

A digital version of this template is available online at www.billzipp.com/salessuccess.

Keep the answers to these questions current, go over them every few weeks or so, and you'll never have another desperate moment where a sales meeting arrives, and you've got nothing to give your team.

Three Kinds of Sales Team Meetings

There are three kinds of team meetings you need to have in the course of a sales year. Each meeting has its own unique purpose and its own distinct vibe. There's the weekly team meeting, the quarterly team meeting, and the annual sales meeting. Here are my thoughts on each:

I. Weekly Team Meetings

Weekly team meetings are the place you'll get to apply the inspiration, instruction, interaction, and information template the most. As with one-on-ones, I recommend having these meetings three times per month and taking the last week of the month off to give folks breathing room. The logic again for this is that most everything in sales has a thirty- to sixty-day echo effect. That is, if you roll something out in a team meeting, that rollout won't impact sales results for another thirty to sixty days. Meeting as a team once a month is too infrequent, especially if a meeting gets missed for some reason. Meeting every other week is too infrequent as well, because every other week meetings quite easily slip into once a month meetings with a sick day, vacation day, or a scheduling conflict, and you'll find yourself with a month—if not a whole quarter—lost forever.

Keep your weekly meetings short and focused. Get in and out in an hour, no longer than seventy-five minutes. If you manage a remote team and meet virtually online, you need to get in and out of your meeting in forty-five minutes or less to keep the attention of your salespeople. This means starting a meeting with five to ten minutes devoted to inspiration, then spending the next thirty to thirty-five minutes providing instruction and engaging in interaction or both at the same time as described above. Then wrapping things up with important information and an opportunity to ask questions about that information. If you're managing this appropriately, it should take ten to fifteen minutes. Do this well thirty-six times per year, and the difference in your team will be dramatic.

Six Essentials for Virtual Meetings

Every sales leader I know conducts some, or even most, of their weekly team meetings online in a virtual environment. This is an inescapable reality in today's business world. Not being live, in-person with your salespeople, however, poses unique challenges for meeting effectiveness and leadership impact. Here are six essentials for overcoming these challenges:

1. Invest in quality technology

The biggest issue I see that undermines the effectiveness of virtual team meetings is doing them on the cheap. Because free, or nearly free, software options exist for conducting meetings online, companies flock to them. But these freemium platforms aren't stable enough for quality interaction and invariably produce an immense amount of frustration. This is, as they say, penny wise and pound foolish. Find a solid, stable platform that won't break up, cut out, or crash completely, and then learn how to use all the platform's features, from polling to breakout rooms, whiteboards to screen sharing. You get what you pay for here.

2. Insist everyone use their video camera

Having a stable meeting platform doesn't mean people will use it. It's too easy to leave the camera off and jump on audio only. Don't let your team do this. Without the accountability of being seen, distractions will lure participants' attention away from the meeting every time. Get face-to-face-to-face-to-face without exception in your online meetings.

3. Call on people by name

This is a counterintuitive practice that only applies to virtual meetings. At an in-person meeting when you call on a person out-of-the-blue by name, it can be seen as rude and aggressive. In a virtual meeting, it's essential for keeping people's attention and preventing long, awkward gaps of silence. Establish this practice as a clear expectation for all of your virtual meetings. Explain why you're doing it, then dive in, graciously yet firmly. I'll often use a variation of this in my virtual meetings by having the first person I call on by name pick the next person to speak, then that person picks the next person, and so on. This way I'm not always the bad guy. Here's the bottom line on this: if I'm in a virtual meeting and I know that at any time the leader will call on me by name, you can bet I'm paying attention!

4. Keep the numbers small

Which brings up another virtual team meeting essential. If time doesn't allow you to call on the participants in your meeting multiple times by name, that meeting has too many people in it. Sure, technology exists for hundreds of people to attend an online meeting all at the same time. But your sales team meetings have a different purpose: connection and interaction, not the mass dissemination of information. That's why I recommend eight or fewer in attendance so no one can hide. At an in-person meeting, you can run your eyes around the room and make eye contact with everyone present. You can't do this in a virtual meeting, so keep the numbers small.

5. Make your meetings short and fast-paced

Distractions do exist in a virtual meeting environment, much more than live, in-person, so you've got to keep your meetings short and you've got to keep them moving. As I mentioned above, a virtual meeting should be forty-five minutes or less—no longer than an hour. Shortness, however, is just one part of the equation. Virtual meetings have got to move at a faster pace than in-person meetings, again because of the distractions inherent in them. This means having lots of people participating in your meetings, having fun throughout them, and not getting off track. Listen to a morning radio show on your drive to work one day. That's the kind of thing I'm talking about. These DJ's know that at any second a listener can turn them off or jump to another channel. This is true about your reps as well. Steal a few ideas from these professional communicators and amp up your virtual meetings.

6. Get in-person at least once a quarter

Finally, there's no substitute for being live, in-person. Business realities may not allow this every week, but at least once a quarter get eyeball-to-eyeball with your salespeople. That may mean bringing them to you or your going to them, but without live connection, drift will inevitably occur. That remote salesperson who used to hit her number every month, slowly becomes missing in action, then mysteriously starts working for the competition. Ouch! But that's how the universe works, proceeding from order to disorder. Wise leaders reverse this trend by injecting meaningful, in-person contact.

II. Quarterly Team Meetings

The temptation in your weekly meetings is trying to do too much in them. That is, attempting to discuss big picture, 30,000-foot issues, addressing sweeping organizational changes, or providing in-depth sales training. The weekly meeting is too short, and the time pressure of a typical sales week too intense, to do any of these effectively. That's what a quarterly team meeting is for.

Quarterly team meetings are typically off-site for a day or a day-and-a-half. Although I use the word quarterly, the most I've seen this done is three times a year, with the annual meeting, discussed below, replacing one of the quarters. Just as with a weekly team meeting, use the inspiration, instruction, interaction, and information template, but expand one or two of these elements significantly, like instruction or interaction. The dynamics of hanging out together for an extended period of time tend to spark inspiration on its own, but dinner and drinks in the evening can make the day extra special. Because you're taking your salespeople out of the field, however, make sure to deliver overwhelming value during the day.

Budget considerations are the primary constraint in planning quarterly meetings. While it's fun to go to super cool places, that can get expensive. Almost always, there are just as cool local hangouts that don't cost an arm and a leg to rent (or travel to). One of the best quarterly meetings I ever attended was in the cellar of a regional winery where we ended the day tasting wine and sampling local meats and cheeses. And the best part? The wine cellar got terrible cell coverage, so we weren't interrupted the entire day.

Quarterly Sprints

A powerful twist on the quarterly meeting is the quarterly sprint. Quarterly sprints take the sales year, and, instead of having just one finish line in December, create four finish lines at the end of each quarter, or four 12 week "years."

Quarterly sprints recognize that deadlines drive behavior change, who among us would complete our taxes apart from an April 15 deadline? I shopped online for a present for my wife late last night so it would arrive at our house in time for our anniversary. Deadlines. Drive. Behavior change.

Quarterly sprints also cooperate with human nature. They recognize that deadlines with shorter time frames are more effective than deadlines with longer time frames, because, like yours truly running a half-marathon, we tend to lose our way when finish lines are too far from sight.

Finally, quarterly sprints provide flexibility within your sales year. Every sales year I've experienced had unique twists and turns that a one-year plan couldn't predict. Quarterly sprints, however, allow you to pivot your plan to meet marketplace challenges.

How Do You Conduct a Quarterly Sprint?

Here are four practices I've found beneficial in helping my clients implement quarterly sprints:

1. Pick a Theme

Periodization. That's what endurance athletes call what I've been referring to here as quarterly sprints. An athlete preparing for a triathlon, for instance, would run, cycle, and swim continuously, but for one period of time—about eight to twelve weeks—she would put greater emphasis on one of those activities, expanding strength in that area and preparing her to compete at the highest level of excellence. Periodization has become the gold standard for training endurance athletes. It should be your gold standard in leading sales professionals.

Picking a theme for a quarterly sprint involves selecting a strategic activity in your sales process you want to emphasize in a twelve-week period of time.

For example, a first quarter sprint could focus on building pipeline and a fourth quarter sprint could focus on closing open opportunities. A second quarter sprint could focus on deepening partner relationships and a third quarter sprint could focus on expanding business with existing customers (or anything else that makes sense).

Just like triathletes, your salespeople continue to execute the steps of your sales process, but the emphasis on one key activity allows you to expand your team's strength in that area. It also equips them to compete in the marketplace at the highest level of excellence.

2. Run a Contest

Now that you've picked a theme for a quarterly sprint, it's time to have some fun with it. Run a contest! What a contest does is track and reward performance for the sales activity that's the focus of a quarterly sprint. A well-run contest has weekly individual and team winners, monthly individual and team winners. Then, of course, it recognizes quarterly overall winners as well.

For example, if for the second quarter of the year, you want to emphasize utilizing partner relationships in generating and closing deals, you could run a contest around:

- The number of partner meetings scheduled
- The number of partner leads shared
- The amount of appointments scheduled due to a partner lead
- The amount of partner generated deals closed
- The largest partner generated deal closed

A contest like this has plenty of things to track and plenty of milestones to celebrate, injecting enthusiasm into the quarter and strengthening the partner muscles of your sales team.

I usually make the rewards I distribute during my quarterly sprints more about pride than money. I suggest you do the same. Give away simple prizes and affordable gift cards, celebrating together as a group at the end of the quarter with a fun team-building event. Spend your big dollars on comp and commission.

3. Take a Break

Yes, take a break. Salespeople can get contest fatigue and burn out completely if you don't provide some rest from sprinting. The rhythm of a quarter allows for this with twelve weeks on and one week off. Some quarters have natural breaks for holidays and vacations. Often I'll take three to four weeks off from a contest and run a quarterly sprint for only eight to ten weeks.

Again, these aren't weeks where your salespeople stop selling. Neither are they weeks where you skip your one-on-one's, forecast calls, and team meetings. They're just weeks where you're taking a break from the overlay of a quarterly sprint to this specific period of time.

4. Rinse and Repeat

Like anything in life, quarterly sprints are a skill that must be learned. The first one or two my clients conduct usually have mixed results. That's okay. Rinse and repeat. In other words, learn from each quarterly sprint. Keep what worked, get rid of what didn't, and move on.

That's another great benefit of quarterly sprints, more frequent assessment and analysis. Asking, "What worked?" "What didn't work?" and "What can we do better?" is a good thing to do at the end of every sales year, but all too often it's too late to do anything about the answers to those questions.

Quarterly sprints followed by quarterly assessment and analysis quickly closes the learning gap and helps your sales team get better faster. Imagine learning what's working with partnerships, what's not working with partnerships, and fixing it early in the sales year rather than waiting until after the year is over and quota is missed (again). That's what quarterly sprints provide you.

III. Annual Sales Meetings

The annual sales meeting is a way to put the inspiration, instruction, interaction, and information template on steroids. The temptation, when you spend the time and money to bring everyone together once a year, is to err on the side of information. This kind of meeting, however, is a perfect opportunity for fulfilling other priorities. The crude warning to sellers on a first call applies here: Don't show up and throw up. That is, don't use your annual sales meeting for a data dump on product, price, promotion, and positioning.

You don't have to ignore important information, but there's a higher priority. Inspiration. The annual meeting is a time to demonstrate genuine appreciation for the hard work salespeople have given your company in the past year. It's time to deepen the personal connections that will keep the fires burning next year and mend a few fences that may have become frayed last year. And yes, it's time to recognize and reward the individuals and teams that have been the best of the best. A winning sales culture freely celebrates excellence, and in the celebration, duplicates that excellence exponentially.

This focused time away is tailor-made for instruction as well. Make sure, however, as discussed above, that the content is extremely interactive, because that's how salespeople learn. Don't jam them into a room and talk incessantly (show up, and you know…). Also, make sure instruction is aligned with your sales process and any product rollouts you have planned in the coming months.

Finally, follow through. Effective equipping of a sales force is more like a soaker hose than a firehose. The annual sales meeting is a firehose. There's really no way around it. But follow-up your annual meeting with a drip system that revisits everything you covered in it. In other words, soaker hose your sales force. That's the only way to make things stick. Remember: over-communicate by a factor of ten.

Meetings, meetings, meetings, meetings. You're probably sick of sitting in meetings. I'm sure your salespeople are as well. Some estimates put sales meeting attendance as high as forty hours every month. That's an entire workweek spent in meetings every thirty days. The answer to this dilemma is not less meetings, but better meetings (okay, maybe a few less meetings) and shorter meetings. Meetings that deliver value every time. Meetings that help your salespeople make more money. Now go do it!

PART III
MULTIPLICATION

"No company can grow revenue consistently faster than its ability to get enough of the right people to implement that growth ... It is one thing above all others: get and keep the right people."[5]
—Jim Collins

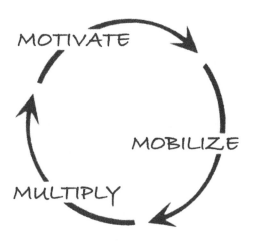

Chapter Ten
HIRING

I t's one of the goofiest things that's ever happened to me. In the course of my sales consulting career, I've helped many of my clients hire candidates for open sales seats at their company. I've read thousands of resumes and conducted hundreds of interviews, but this one was "special."

First, he arrived late. "Car trouble," he said. We could tell too. His beat-up Chevy was still smoking from its drive on the freeway to our offices. He looked like a hippie from the sixties, but that's kind of normal for the Pacific Northwest. It was an inside sales job, so the ponytail and the hemp wouldn't be that big of a deal if he could sell.

But then it happened. Halfway through the interview, he pulled a banana from his pants pocket. Yes, a banana … from his pants pocket.

"I'm hypoglycemic," he said, "and need to eat something."

Peeling the skin from the banana (did I mention it came from his pants pocket?), he reached out to me and asked, "Wanna bite?"

I passed. And so did we in moving forward with this job applicant.

Fortunately, or perhaps, unfortunately as we'll see in a minute, most candidates interviewing for an open sales position don't act this way. In fact, they act just the opposite. Most candidates for an open sales position, being salespeople, present well in an interview. Any interview. Because that's what salespeople do. Give them a stage, and they're ready to perform. With some salespeople, the best work you'll ever get out of them begins and ends with the interview.

Which makes hiring good salespeople notoriously difficult. Statistics bear this out. If you hired five new salespeople today without utilizing any of the principles in this chapter, only one will contribute in a meaningful way to top line revenue, three will become marginal performers, and one will become a total disaster. That's net neutral, and depending on the damage done by the latter, net negative.

It's obvious, right? You can't build a successful sales organization with a 20% hiring retention rate. Here's a better way: five sales hiring mistakes to avoid and five sales hiring practices to follow.

Hiring Mistake One: Falling in Love with One Person

This is by far the biggest sales hiring mistake I see leaders making. You meet a person, you like a person, and you become convinced this person would be perfect for an open sales position at your company. "I feel it in my gut," you say. You've got great instincts about people, right?

So, you hire this person, and guess what? It doesn't work out. Why? To turn a phrase slightly, because love is blind, and hiring is an eye-opener.

When you fall in love with someone, a romantic prospect or an employment prospect, you don't see his or her faults, and with stars in your eyes, believe that everything will work out. Love will find a way! Alas, at least when it comes to hiring, it does not.

Here's your alternative. Start by defining the open sales position you want to fill. Clearly outline the responsibilities of the role and the specific, measurable outcomes associated with those responsibilities. Armed with these metrics, pursue a rigorous, data-driven process for finding a great fit, matching past sales performance with these measurable outcomes. Moneyball for sales selection.

What do you do with the people you fall in love with and want to hire? Encourage them to apply for the job and ask them to go through the process like everyone else. In this way, sales hiring becomes an objective, results-driven system, not subjective, gut-feel emotional guesswork.

Hiring Mistake Two: Fishing in Too Small a Pond

This second sales hiring mistake is a lot like the first one, the flip side of the same coin. Instead of falling in love with one person, with this mistake you have only a handful of people from which to choose and pick the candidate who offers the least possible downside. That's no way to build a team of world-class sales professionals. A deep pool of candidates offers you many options and an opportunity to pick the brightest and best.

How in the world do you achieve this, especially if unemployment is low? In a word, culture. Culture is the key to successful sales hiring today. Becoming a place people want to work at, a place people love coming to on Monday morning (or any other day of the week). In short, becoming an employer of choice.

Just like when prospecting, where the best new customers come from existing customers who are thrilled with your work, the best new salespeople come from existing salespeople who are thrilled with their work. When you have a culture like that, resumes pour in for open seats and new hires count their lucky stars to be selected by you.

The added benefit of having a great sales culture is this: when you attract top talent to your team, you'll also retain that talent, reducing turnover and the need to hire for the same position over and over again. You'll also drastically reduce expenses related to recruiting, interviewing, selecting, and onboarding.

Still concerned about culture? Re-read Chapter Five.

Hiring Mistake Three: Accepting Resumes at Face Value

Speaking of resumes, accepting them at face value is sales hiring mistake number three.

Yes, I know, the tried and true hiring document is the resume. but with downloadable templates and resume writing services, most resumes are not what they seem. Not that people are lying, it's just that they're putting the best face on their employment history, and you've got to get below that facade, injecting truth serum into your sales hiring process.

The truth serum I use is the *Career History Form*® from Topgrading. This is a legal, binding document, which a candidate completes online and signs. It asks for all of a person's work history, the names of former supervisors, reasons for leaving every job, and more. I've used this document literally hundreds of times and do not receive one penny from Topgrading as an affiliate or reseller. It's just one of the most effective sales hiring tools on the market today.

What do I do with resumes? I collect them at the front end of the hiring process. They tell me how technologically savvy candidates are and how well they use the English language. I score each resume based on a match with the position profile I created to avoid Hiring Mistake One and send candidates a link to complete the *Career History Form*®. I base the rest of my interactions with them off that form alone and not their resume.

In other words, a resume is a ticket to enter the theater, but it doesn't get a person on stage for an audition. A completed *Career History Form*® and a solid phone screen interview do that.

Hiring Mistake Four: Asking About the Hypothetical Future

That's the first of the three interviews to use in the sales hiring process: the phone screen interview I just mentioned. The other three are The Chronological Interview, The Round Robin Interview, and The Reference Interview. I address each later in the chapter, but the key in all of these interviews is behavior-based inquiry—asking questions, and only questions, about a person's actual past actions.

Most job interviewing is focused on the hypothetical future, "What would you do if…" The hypothetical future tells you nothing about a candidate except how well that person can guess the answers you're looking for. Neither does it predict performance. Only the past does that, because the future is an extension of the past, especially in sales. The opposite of asking questions about the hypothetical future is using historical-behavioral interviewing techniques. Although that sounds like a mouthful, it's simply asking a candidate about the sales activity he or she has completed in previous sales roles.

Here's an example of this approach. Imagine you're hiring a salesperson for a hunter role on your team. That role, as you've defined it, requires setting a certain number of first appointments by making a high volume of outbound cold calls to new prospects. The following are questions you could ask to uncover whether or not a candidate has the skill to succeed this role:

Sales Skill: Set five first appointments per week by making ten outbound calls per day

Interviewing Questions:

1. When you sold for XYZ Company, how did you set appointments with prospects?

2. How many appointments did you set in a typical day? Typical week? Typical month?

3. How would you go about discovering the right people to be calling on at a company?

4. How did you uncover any referral relationships that existed at a company?

5. When you made contact by email, what did a typical email look like? How did you write the subject line? How did you address the recipient? What was a typical first sentence? What did the rest of the email sound like? How did you close the email?

6. What reasons would you give in an email for a prospect to give up their time to meet with you?

7. How frequently did you email your prospects? Did you change the email each time you sent it, or…? How many email contacts did you make in a day? What was your success rate at getting first appointments by email?

8. When you made contact by phone, what did a typical conversation sound like? What were the first words out of your mouth? How did you deal with prospects who wanted to hang up on you? If you got voice mail, did you leave a message? Why? What did it sound like?

9. How frequently do you think a salesperson should phone their prospects? How many dials do you like to make in a day?

10. What was your success rate at getting first appointments by phone? What reasons did you give on the phone for a prospect to give up their time to meet with you?

11. This is hard work, and sometimes very discouraging, how did you stay motivated?

12. What other sales or marketing methods did you use to connect with your prospects and set appointments? What were your favorites? What were your least favorites?

13. How did you decide when it was time to move on from a prospect and work on a better opportunity? What were your account management strategies?

14. What did you love about making cold calls for XYZ Company? What did you hate about it?

The pushback I usually get when I talk about conducting a ninety-minute Chronological Interview, as I'll recommend below, is this, "What in the world do you talk about during that time?" But notice, all fourteen questions above are related to just one sales skill. In fact, including follow-up queries for further clarification, there are a total of thirty-five questions in that list. Let's assume you have five core sales skills aligned with your job profile. That's 175 questions to ask in ninety minutes. See how the time can fly by?

By the way, don't ignore Question 11 and Question 14. These questions concerning a candidate's inner world related to a core sales skill will predict performance much more than any personality test. If one person's answer to Questions 14 is, "I just loved our cold calling days. I made a game out of it and played to win!" and another's is, "I hated our cold calling days. My stomach was always tied up in knots, and I couldn't wait until it was time to go home," which of these candidates will do well in a hunter role?

Real Work Alert

Pull out the profile you created for the open sales position on your team. You did that, right, to avoid Sales Hiring Mistake One? List the sales skills needed to achieve the outcomes you've set for success in the role. Now create historical-behavioral interviewing questions for each skill.

Sales Skill One:

Interviewing Questions:

Sales Skill Two:

Interviewing Questions:

Sales Skill Three:

Interviewing Questions:

Sales Skill Four:

Interviewing Questions:

Sales Skill Five:

Interviewing Questions:

A digital version of this template is available online at www.billzipp.com/salessuccess.

Hiring Mistake Five: Not Screening for Cultural Fit

The final sales hiring mistake is screening for skills only and not for the values that are at the heart of your company's culture.

Skills are important, yes. You don't want to hire a salesperson who can't use the phone to set appointments or a bookkeeper who can't balance a checking account. And no, some skills can't be taught to good people. I can't balance my checkbook to save my life, and no one taught me how to use the phone to set appointments. I just did. So it's not an either/or choice—job skills *or* cultural fit—it's a both/and choice, job skills *and* cultural fit.

Which means you need to know the values at the heart of your company's culture and the behaviors that demonstrate those values in real life. This takes a bit of work, but it's worth it. Now, without tipping your hand (as in, "Tell me about a time you showed integrity." You've got to be shrewder than that.), ask about situations in a candidate's past where these values were put to the test (as in, "Tell me about a time when you made a big mistake with a client. How did you discover it and what did you do to fix it?")

Four Interviews and One Best Practice

In addition to avoiding the five mistakes above to hire good salespeople almost every time, it's critical to use four different kinds of interviews and to apply one best practice to the process. These are:

Hiring Interview One: The Phone Screen Interview

The collection of resumes from a job posting triggers the use of Topgrading's *Career History Form®*, as I mentioned above. But about half of the candidates you ask to complete a *Career History Form®* won't. Why? The form itself acts as a screening process that begins to uncover the best of the best. Certain people won't divulge the kind of information you're asking for, and you don't want those people selling for you.

Work through the *Career History Forms®* you receive and decide which candidates you want to move forward with. A top ten list, of sorts, and proceed to the The Phone Screen Interview.

What you want to do in The Phone Screen Interview is to talk briefly with the people on your top ten list and see if it makes sense to ask them to participate in a more in-depth discussion. Ask these questions in this order, according to *The A-Method of Hiring* designed by ghSmart and Associates:

1. What are your career goals?
2. What are you really good at professionally?
3. What are you not so good at, or not interested in doing, professionally?
4. Who were your last three bosses, and how will each rate your performance on a 1-10 scale when we talk to them?[16]

And, of course, listen. Really listen. Double and triple click on the question to get to the truth below the surface.

Good phone screen interviewing will get you down to three or four finalists that you'll meet with face-to-face and complete the next two kinds of interviews, The Chronological Interview and The Round Robin Interview. These interviews, as you'll see in a bit, are a significant investment of time, so make sure your phone screen skills are sharp. Close your eyes, if you have to, and focus on vocal tone and pace, personal energy, and confidence. That's how this person will sound when they're on the phone with your prospects and customers. Do they have the right stuff?

Hiring Interview Two: The Chronological Interview

The Chronological Interview is based on the simple premise that the past is the best predictor of the future, not a personality profile. In his book, *Topgrading*, Brad Smart extensively documents this premise and presents the Chronological Interview as the key to hiring success, a "silver bullet" as he refers to it.[17]

In a Chronological Interview you ask these seven questions to every finalist about every job they have ever worked, using behavior-based questions to drill down on the details:

1. What were you hired to do?
2. What were your responsibilities?

3. What were your successes in this job and how did you achieve them?
4. What were your failures?
5. Who was your boss and what were his/her strengths and weaker points?
6. What's your best guess as to what your boss will tell me were your strengths and weaker points?
7. Why did you leave this job?[18]

Expect to spend about seventy-five to ninety minutes per interview and be prepared to learn more about a candidate than you have ever learned through any other interviewing methodology.

I've personally conducted hundreds of chronological interviews, and each one is incredibly revealing. I tell candidates that I'm not playing gotcha. That is, I'm not trying to trap them with a question to embarrass them or ask something incredibly lame, like, "Sell me this pen." I tell the people I'm interviewing that I'm looking for themes in their work history and style—how they like to be managed and how they get things done—seeking to discover if those themes fit the style and culture they might be joining. Everyone wants a job for which they feel like they're a good fit. Finding that fit is the point of all of these interviews.

A best practice in conducting Chronological Interviews is to do them in tandem, using two people to interview one candidate. This brings two sets of eyes, two sets of ears, and two perspectives to the table, not just one. A slick salesperson may fool you—a busy leader— but usually can't fool your battle-hardened assistant. Or both of you at the same time. Right?

Hiring Interview Three: The Round Robin Interview

The third of the four interviews is The Round Robin Interview. I say third provisionally because it clearly comes after The Phone Screen

Interview, but it can be done in conjunction with The Chronological Interview.

I usually set up an interviewing day where one kind of interview is going on while the other is also going on at the same time, debriefing the observations of everyone involved at the end of the day. On the same day I conduct a Chronological Interview, candidate finalists—before or after their Chronological Interview—meet with a series of people at the company, individually or as a group, and spend time with them in focused conversation. These people are a cross-section of employees, coworkers, assistants, and supervisors who are instructed to get to know a candidate as best they can in the time allotted them.

The vibe of The Round Robin Interview is very different than the Chronological Interview and even The Phone Screen Interview. The point is not to dig into a person's past, but to see how they handle themselves in the present. Do they look people in the eye? Smile? Remember names? Laugh at themselves? Treat others with respect? While you wouldn't hire someone who nailed the Round Robin Interview but blew the Chronological Interview, the opposite should give you pause. The perspective of your frontline employees is extremely helpful here.

Years ago, Southwest approached this process in a fascinating way. When pilots showed up for a job interview, they first checked in with a receptionist. They were then taken down the hall to another office and another receptionist. A handful of offices and a series of receptionists later, they arrived at the interview but had really been through one already. The people along the way were instructed to note how each pilot conducted himself at every juncture. Pilots, super smart, intense individuals, aren't known for their warmth and friendliness, especially to perceived underlings. Because of their fun-loving, collegial culture, that's not the kind of pilots Southwest wanted working for them. So through the gauntlet they went, a round robin interview on steroids.

Hiring Interview Four: The Reference Interview

We haven't checked references yet, have we? That's because it's the last thing you do. Yes, that's right. Reference checking, because of its time-consuming nature and general ineffectiveness, is the last thing you do in the hiring process. Here's how to do it correctly.

After completing Round Robin and Chronological Interviews, ask the candidates you would consider hiring—and only the candidates you would consider hiring—for references. But you pick the references, not the candidate, based on the supervisors and coworkers you discussed in the Chronological Interview.

Now have the candidates set up the reference calls, not you, having these people call you by a certain day (usually the end of the week). When candidates do this, the chances are better that you'll actually hear the unvarnished truth. Additionally, a candidate's timely completion of this exercise tells you something. Can they use the phone to get people to do stuff for them? A critical sales skill, wouldn't you say?

When a reference calls you, here's what to ask. (Again, as outlined in *The A Method of Hiring*):

1. In what context did you work with this person?
2. What were this person's biggest strengths?
3. What were this person's biggest areas of improvement back then? (The key words "back then" opens the door for honesty)
4. What would you rate his/her overall performance in that job on a 1-10 scale? What about his/her performance causes you to give this rating?
5. The person mentioned that he/she struggled with _____ in that job. Can you tell me more about that? (Again, this question opens the door for honesty.)[19]

The real point of the reference interview is to test theories you've developed regarding this person and to see who follows through on this exercise to ensure you select the very best candidate for your open sales seat. I once had a candidate rock the Chronological Interview, but then, not one reference called us back. As impressed as we were with her ability to make a first impression, the lack of follow-through cost her the job.

Best Practice: Complete a Project

Many times, after conducting the four interviews above, candidates will emerge who are virtually equal in competence and experience. How do you break the tie? A project. Even without a tie, a real-life work project reveals what a candidate is truly made of, helping you in your hiring decision

What do I mean by a project? A project is a reasonable field work assignment that demonstrates a candidate's relevant sales skills and abilities. Again, it's designed for this person to shine, not to embarrass them in any way. In other words, it's reasonable. But it's also something real you can use to discern development. It's relevant. Here are some examples:

- Sort through a list of leads and identify which are Class A, Class B, and Class C prospects for your firm.
- Write and send a series of six outbound emails to a new prospect, introducing the salesperson to this prospect and making the case for a live meeting.
- Write and leave a series of three voicemail messages, introducing the salesperson to a new prospect and making the case for a live meeting.
- Conduct an interview with a new prospect about their need for a product or service this candidate is familiar with.

- Make a public presentation using a PowerPoint slide deck for a product or service this candidate is familiar with.

The prospects mentioned above, of course, are pre-selected. I've used real clients posing as prospects or employees doing the same. But field work like this, unlike a job shadow or ride-along, reveals exactly what you've got in a candidate.

What's the Point of All of This?

The most popular science class in my high school was oceanography. The class could only be taken by seniors, and it had the prerequisite of a B or higher in prior science classes. In spite of that, it was packed every year, with students on a waiting list dying to get in.

The reason for its popularity was simple. In the last quarter of the school year, the entire oceanography class went to Baja, Mexico for a week-long extended science experience. The year I went, there was lots of experience and very, very little science. See why the class was popular?

One of the actual science activities we did on the trip was pour a bucket of dirt from our beachfront campground through a series of screen grates, analyzing the results. The screens on the grates became smaller and smaller until only the finest sand could sift through. We then studied the contents of each grate to determine the geological developments that brought these contents to our shore.

This is exactly how to hire the very best salespeople for your firm, screening and screening, narrowing the grid of each screen in each step until all but the finest is left. Your first set of screens is the resume, the Career History Form®, and The Phone Screen Interview. Then you conduct a Chronological Interview, Round Robin Interviews, Reference Interviews, and request the completion of a project, a real-world field-work assignment.

Congratulations! What you have left after all this work is the starting point for a world-class sales organization. The best of the best. The finest. That's the point of all of this.

Chapter Eleven

PROMOTING

It makes perfect sense. You're good at sales. Perhaps, even one of the best on your team. So you should be a sales manager. The role comes with more money, greater visibility within the organization, increased power, and prestige. That was my path into sales management and the path of thousands before me. What could possibly go wrong?

Before I answer that question, let me explain the logic of this move. If you're good at sales, other salespeople on your team will respect you. If other salespeople on your team respect you, you'll be accepted as their sales manager. If you're accepted as their sales manager, you'll be able to lead them effectively.

If A equals B, and B equals C, then A equals C. Right?

Here's where the logic falls apart. Being good at sales and being good at sales management are two completely different tasks. While it's true that a sales manager needs to be respected by his or her team, that won't happen if you don't have the natural talent for leading them. In the only chapter I've ever seen on this topic, "So, You Want to Be a Sales Manager?" Benson Smith and Tony Rutigliano write in *Discover Your Sales Strengths*, "No matter what the perks and pay are, you will not find management rewarding unless you are as good or better at it than you are in your current role. Going from being a star sales performer to an average manager is a very unrewarding promotion."[20]

If you are a senior leader considering the promotion of a successful salesperson on your team, and that person doesn't have the natural talent for managing a team, you set in motion a chain reaction of events. None of them are good. One, you remove a successful salesperson from the marketplace, rolling the dice on whether you can duplicate that success in someone else. Two, you place a person who's used to being successful in a position for which they're not a good fit. This lack of alignment leads to frustration and failure, burnout and turnover. And three, the salespeople this person leads also experience frustration and failure because the management they receive is woefully inadequate. One by one, you'll see them slip out the back door and begin selling for your competitor.

The key to multiplying sales success year after year is first, hiring well—the subject of the last chapter—and promoting wisely—the subject of this chapter. Then making sure the people on your team don't derail in their roles—the subject of the next chapter. Based on two decades of working in the field, here are five critical questions to consider before accepting a promotion from being an individual sales contributor to being a sales manager. Although this book is written for sales managers and not salespeople, I think the questions are most powerful when the "you" being addressed is a salesperson considering a promotion, not a sales manager in role. Encourage candidates under consideration to read this chapter or flip it around in your own head for the people you're considering for promotion.

1. Do you love to sell or do you love to lead?

Birds fly. Fish swim. Rabbits run. It's not just what they do, it's what they love. Ask a bird to swim, a fish to run, and a rabbit to fly, and, well, you've got a problem. This first question, in fact the first three questions about whether you should consider being a sales manager, addresses the kind of things you love to do. Not tolerate or endure but truly, deeply love. These are the things you were created to do, and any promotion you accept should be fully aligned with them.

Answering these questions, however, takes a fair amount of self-awareness, if not brutal honesty. A few years ago, I attended a leadership conference in Miami. At a mid-morning coffee break, I went to the restroom and encountered a line the proverbial mile long. So I shot behind a curtain or two, across the lobby, around a hallway, and found a men's room with no line. As I walked through the double doors, I entered a palatial expanse as big as my house. There was only one person in this real man's men's room, and we met each other eye-to-eye. It was Dan Marino. Yes, *that* Dan Marino, all-Pro, Hall of Fame, 61,000-passing-yards Dan Marino.

Dan smiled at me and said, "Hey!"

I smiled back, cool as a cucumber, and replied, "Hey!" and he went out the door.

Here's what I remember most about that encounter. When I looked Dan Marino in the eyes, I noticed that we're about the same height, about the same weight, and about the same build. I said to myself, "I could have been Dan Marino." Well, except for a few things. I can't throw a football in a tight spiral with pinpoint accuracy fifty yards down a football field. I can't read complex defensive schemes. (I could tell you what a nickel and dime package is, but I never see it on TV unless someone draws those squiggly lines on a monitor.) And I can't release a forward pass in less than three seconds while dodging 300-pound linebackers. Except for those things, I could be Dan Marino.

Those things, however, are the whole point, aren't they? They make Dan Marino *Dan Marino* ... or any successful NFL quarterback. Just a few moments of self-awareness (admittedly, not my greatest strength) and I could see that. Here's what makes a successful salesperson. They love the hunt. They love the challenge of prospecting, and they love the thrill of closing. This is the air they breathe, the water in which they swim, the way they run, and they wouldn't have it any other way.

Do you love sales to that degree? If you do, you may not make the best sales manager because you'll always check yourself into the game to take the final shot, stunting the growth of your sales team. You'll always hijack a sales call so you can feel what it's like to close a big deal again, frustrating recruits and seasoned sellers alike. Here's the first truth about being a sales manager: sales management is *not* selling, it's helping others sell. This isn't a cute play on words but actual reality. Can you give up the thrill of the hunt for the thrill of helping others hunt *without regret?*

Forgive the sports analogy, but are you Dan Marino or are you Don Shula? Both were part of an epic Miami Dolphin run, and both are enshrined in pro football's Hall of Fame, but they did two totally different jobs. One was a quarterback and the other was a coach. What job were you created for? Think about it.

2. Do you love the process or do you love people?

The second part of the Dan Marino or Don Shula, player or coach question is this: Are you a people person or are you a process person? You can succeed in sales, even succeed wildly in sales, by following a defined process. You interact with people, yes, but those interactions don't dominate your day. They serve to move deals along in the process, a process that you love executing from start to finish.

Sales management isn't like that at all. It's people intensive, where process is secondary. The process is always there, of course, behind the scenes, like banks on a river, but the water in the river is the relationships that flow all throughout the day. Do you love a constant stream of conversation that connects you with others from the beginning of your workday until the end? Do these interactions give you energy, or do they leave you exhausted? Do you like to "Slack" or do you find it a nuisance? Sales management is a people first position, and you must love people to excel in it.

By the way, there's no right or wrong answers to these questions. It's not right to be a people person and wrong to be a process person. It's who you are and how you're wired. What becomes right and what becomes wrong is accepting a promotion for a role that's not a fit with your innate talent and natural abilities. Like tires on a car that are out of alignment, you'll wear out and, maybe even, blowout driving down the wrong road for you.

3. Do you love the spotlight or can you work on the sidelines?

Here's another area where you should be brutally honest with yourself. Why do you sell? In Chapter Three we discussed that people choose a career in sales for four distinct reasons: fortune, fame, freedom, and family. For those whose primary motivation is fame, success in sales is not about the money. It's about what the money means, not becoming a media darling but receiving personal attention and public recognition. A person who sells for fame loves being on top of the leaderboard, being awarded prizes in front of their peers and being praised by their supervisors. This means that if you choose to become a sales manager, you're consciously choosing to step out of that spotlight and letting it shine brightly on others who sell for you. Can you do that? If you sell for fame, maybe not.

In addition, as we discussed in Chapter Four, because of the sales persona, a tendency to extroversion that comes with a dependency on energy coming from the outside in, and because of the sales profession, always living in the land of no, salespeople are always in need of praise. They need a manager who takes every opportunity to recognize and reward their activity. Can you do that day in and day out? And can you do that if no one recognizes and rewards you?

Bottom line: To do your best work, do you need to be on stage in the spotlight receiving the applause of the crowd, or are you just as happy offstage, on the sidelines directing the play from behind the scenes, receiving no, or very little, public acclamation? Again, there's no right answer or no wrong answer here. It's just the honest reality of what the role of sales manager entails and how your abilities align with that role.

4. Do you communicate cross-functionally or does that leave you exhausted?

Let's shift gears now from love to loathe, okay? The first three questions we've been discussing in considering a promotion from individual sales contributor to sales manager have to do with the kind of things that give you energy. This question has to do with the kind of things that take it away and leave you feeling exhausted. Loathing something is just as much an indicator of an innate ability—that is, the lack thereof—as loving something. So consider with me for a moment your enthusiasm for cross-functional communication.

Individual sales contributors rarely interact with other parts of the business. Sure, it happens, but it's not too common an occurrence. When it happens, it often does not go well because salespeople are a bit more intense and competitive than people who work in other parts of the business. And usually that's okay. Most of their coworkers get it. The hunters get cranky sometimes, but at the end of the day, we all get to eat.

Sales managers, however, cannot behave this way. Much of their job involves interacting cross-functionally within the organization. They talk to marketing about inbound leads from the website and outbound calling campaigns. They talk to implementation about accelerating the deployment of a complex deal. They talk to human resources about sharing commission between two aggressive reps. On and on the list goes. Much of a sales manager's success depends on his or her ability to represent the team to other parts of the business well.

So the question for you is this. Can you do this? Not just do it occasionally but day in and day out? When you communicate cross-functionally in the organization, does it energize you or leave you completely exhausted? Do you refer to this kind of activity as political rear end kissing? Do you loathe a core element of what it takes to be successful in the role of sales manager? If you do, stay away. It will destroy both you and the people with whom you work.

5. Do you leave on Friday afternoon or do you work the weekend?

What do you love? What do you loathe? And now, what's your lifestyle? That's the focus of this final question. Are you at a place in your life where the extra time it takes to be a sales manager is available to you? This is what I mean by asking about leaving on Friday afternoon versus working the weekend. Not a perfect set of words, I know. But let me explain...

Every successful salesperson I know disappears on Friday afternoon to get a head start on the weekend. And people look the other way. No problem, they're above goal, they always hit their number, and they always make club. Part of what fuels their success, in fact, is an endless array of outside interests that require long weekends to pursue, whether it be family activities, flipping houses, or extreme sports. The freedom of sales fuels their commitment to it. They work hard and they play hard.

That kind of freedom, however, is only available to individual contributors. Sales managers need to be available to all their sellers, the high performers and the low performers (who can't afford to skip any part of any day of the week) and to their managers (who tend to reach out to them at oddball times, like Friday afternoons). Consequently, sales managers can't leave early on Friday afternoon and often find themselves working on the weekend. But they don't mind it because that's what they love. Really. They love the interaction that comes from working with a team. It gives them energy. They love doing whatever it takes to transform the careers of the people who work for them. They love building something meaningful and significant. Do you?

Lifestyle issues also include a marriage, a divorce, the birth or adoption of a child, a bad health diagnosis, the death of a spouse, or an aging parent. All kinds of life circumstances make the time needed for effective sales management harder to come by and the freedom of being an individual contributor liberating. Think these through seriously. Life is more than work.

Real Work Alert

I've placed the questions discussed above as sets of contrasting pairs in the assessment below. Rate each contrasting pair for yourself, or for someone you're considering for sales management. The rating of 0 in the middle indicates no preference for one statement over the other, and the ratings of 1, 2, or 3 in either direction indicates to what degree a preference exists, 3 being the highest for either. After rating each pair, total the score for Column A, the numbers selected to the left of the 0 in the middle, and total the score for Columns B, the numbers selected to the right of the 0 in the middle. Now subtract Column A's total from Column B's total. Place that number in the bottom square labeled Overall Total.

When you complete this exercise, you'll have a sense of a person's preference for being and independent sales contributor or being a sales manager. It's a little simplistic, I know, but it gives you something to openly discuss, as opposed to moving forward thoughtlessly with a promotion. By the way, I don't recommend moving forward unless a person's overall total is 8 or higher.

Column A	Rating							Column B
You love to sell.	3	2	1	0	1	2	3	You love to lead.
You love the sales process.	3	2	1	0	1	2	3	You love people.
You love the spotlight.	3	2	1	0	1	2	3	You can work on the sidelines.
Cross-functional communication exhausts you.	3	2	1	0	1	2	3	You communicate well cross-functionally.
You work hard to leave early on Friday afternoon.	3	2	1	0	1	2	3	You like to work on the weekend.
TOTAL: *Numbers to the left of 0*								**TOTAL:** *Numbers to the right of 0*

Subtract Column A's Total from Column B's Total	OVERALL TOTAL:

**A digital version of this assessment is available online at
www.billzipp.com/salessuccess.**

Again, I thought these statements were most powerful when presented in the second person, as if you were a salesperson considering a promotion to sales manager. But you're already a sales manager, so maybe your score explains the frustration you're experiencing in the role right now. Think through each pair. Where can you make some changes? Would it be better for you to return to selling? I know more than a few former sales leaders who wisely—and courageously, I might add—decided that it simply wasn't in their DNA to be a manager. You can't put in what God left out. Be true to who you are.

A promotion from individual sales contributor to sales manager is not always the right move. It works for some, and it's a total disaster for others. Make sure this position is a good fit for you or the person you're considering for management—what you love, what you loathe, and what's your lifestyle—before moving forward. Your future self will thank me later.

Chapter Twelve
DERAILING

We have a long-standing Thanksgiving tradition in our house. I cook the food and my wife cleans up. She's not fond of the laborious preparation a full turkey dinner takes, and I, being male, am not fond of cleaning. It's a trade-off that works for both of us. As I'm preparing dinner, the rest of the family sits at the kitchen table and plays cards, jawing at each other. It's a fun family festivity.

A couple of years ago, after I peeled ten pounds of potatoes (there's never enough mashed potatoes at our dinner table), the drain that flowed from the sink into the garbage disposal and out became clogged. Too many tiny potatoes peels plugged the pipe and backed up the drain. It being Thanksgiving Day and all, no plumber on earth was available.

No plumber? No problem!

I'd read an article on the Internet for a situation just like this. I took our toilet plunger and plunged the opening of the garbage disposal. The article on the Internet said the pressure of the plunger would break up the clog of potato peels and blow the water through the drain.

Pretty cool, huh? And that's exactly what it did. Here's what else it did. The pressure was so intense that it burst all the joints of our drainpipes below the sink, flooding the kitchen with dirty sink water and endless scraps of potato peels. Thanksgiving would never be the same.

This silly story perfectly parallels what can happen in a sales leader's life. Everything is going along fine until some problem occurs. An unexpected turnover, the loss of a major client, or missed quota for the quarter. You name it, and the pressure starts to build. Like a plunger forcing water through the pipes of your life, something blows and there's a mess everywhere. Over the course of two decades working with sales leaders, I've seen many of these meltdowns occur. They're entirely preventable. How? By making sure the joints, the most vulnerable areas of your leadership, are strong and secure.

In other words, you can hire and promote the right people, placing them in the perfect role. But those same people, including you, can blow out of that role—making a big fat mess for everyone to clean up. Here are three common sales leadership derailers and how to keep them from sabotaging you: manic mornings, the myth of multitasking, and working on the weekend.

Derailer One: Manic Mornings

There she sat across the table from me. Frazzled, frustrated, and utterly exhausted. This gifted, passionate leader had been the CEO of her company for only a few months, but she was already running on empty. And wondering…

Wondering if the role was right for her. Wondering if she had what it takes to lead at this level. Wondering if all her hard work really mattered anyway. Yes, yes, and yes. But no. No to how she was going about it: waking up, smartphone in hand, texting, emailing, and getting the latest news before her first cup of coffee, continuing her mad dash through the day and collapsing in bed just before midnight, smartphone in hand again. This is a recipe for disaster, physically and emotionally, mentally and spiritually. So I shared with her the rules and rhythms of how to win the morning. I now share them with you.

How to Win the Morning: Four Rules

Successful leaders for centuries have made the very first hour of their day a protected, private time for personal reflection and strategic preparation. They do this because they believe that when they win the morning, they also win the day. And when they win the day—everyday—they win the weeks, the months, and the years of their lives and leadership. Whether you're a busy CEO or a stressed-out sales leader, here's my approach to this daily practice.

1. No Snooze

The first key to winning the morning is refusing to lose to your alarm clock. Every time it goes off and you hit snooze, you're admitting defeat at the very start of the day. Rule number one is this: when the alarm clock goes off, get up. No exceptions. No excuses.

What that means for most of us is getting ready to win the morning the night before. Turning off the television, shutting down our electronic devices, not drinking too much alcohol, and going to bed at a decent time. If waking up is a challenge for you, Google the term "sleep hygiene" and follow the instructions you find. Or read the brilliant book *The Promise of Sleep* by a pioneer in sleep research, Dr. William Dement.

2. No News

The second rule involves not injecting yourself with the drug of adrenaline at the very start of the day. "If it doesn't bleed, it doesn't lead," is a newsroom mantra for a reason. News is about the latest emergency. Breaking headlines scream crisis, crisis, crisis. If there's no crisis to report, one will be made up. This is not how you want to begin your day because crisis kills creativity, short-term urgencies undermine long-term priorities. Feel free to read the news later in the day, just don't start with it.

3. No Email

For similar reasons, the first hour of your day should not be spent answering email (or posting on social media). "Once you start looking at email, the whole day cascades into email responses and replying back and forth," writes Laura Vanderkam in *What the Most Successful People Do Before Breakfast.*[21] Urgency, not priority. Crisis, not creativity. Don't start any day this way. Again, after your morning practice, take the time to answer your email, but not before.

4. No Cheating

This final rule is like the eleventh commandment. What's the eleventh commandment? Do the first ten! In other words, don't cheat on these rules. And I know that's easier said than done, adrenaline can become an addiction and checking email an obsession. As with any bad habit, though, its power must be broken or your life is not your own.

How to Win the Morning: Four Rhythms

What do you do instead of reading the news, checking email, and posting on social media first thing in the morning? Here are four rhythms:

1. Read and Reflect

Instead of injecting yourself with a shot of adrenaline, the first thing to do in the morning is read and reflect. Reading and reflection feeds your mind, your nurtures soul, and renews your spirit. That's why it's the first thirty minutes of my morning practice. I read the New Testament, Psalms, and Proverbs in their entirety about once a year and write in my journal the thoughts and prayers that flow from these texts. Your spiritual tradition may be different than mine, but the principle is the same.

2. Exercise

Having fed my soul and spirit, the next thirty minutes of my morning practice involves physical exercise. It doesn't take much, but a half an hour of vigorous exercise, some strength training and stretching, and I'm energized for the day. If I need a longer run or a more extensive workout, I'll do it later in the afternoon or on the weekend. While leaders of past centuries don't mention health club memberships and elliptical machines as part of their morning practice, they didn't live the sedentary sitting life we do today. That's why exercise is the second morning rhythm.

3. Review Your Vision

Now it's time to think about work, but not its pressing problems. Reviewing vision is about looking at your strategic priorities. The demands of the day should always be filtered through a larger lens, the view from 30,000 feet.

"Concentration—that is, the courage to impose what really matters most and comes first—is the executive's only hope of mastering time and events instead of being their whipping boy," Peter Drucker wrote four decades ago in *The Effective Executive*.[22] His words are even more true today. Impose what matters most and comes first by reviewing the vision you have for your life and leadership. What do you really want to achieve and why do you want to achieve it? Live fully aligned with these priorities. In other words, stop being urgency's whipping boy.

4. Plan for Execution

Now you're ready to plan the day, but in a different way than perhaps you're used to. Instead of having a long list of things to do and whacking at that list like a slab of bologna, take a different approach. Ask yourself, "What are the most important things I can do today to fulfill my top priorities?"

Pick five or fewer—three might even be best—and write them down. You can use a three-by-five card, an app on your smartphone, or a dry erasable board on the wall. Whatever method you choose, these five (or fewer) are your focus for the day. I call these items VIT's: Very Important Tasks. They're not the only things you'll do in the day, for sure. But they're the first things you do. The most important things. The things that are aligned with the vision you have for your life and leadership. The cumulative effect of getting five VIT's done without fail has a profound impact on personal and professional productivity. You'll be amazed at the difference the execution of a vital few priorities every day will have on your success as a leader, instead of trying to do a dozen things in a day that only get done half-way.

Derailer Two: The Myth of Multitasking

I just landed at O'Hare airport in Chicago. After getting off the airplane, I ordered an Uber, read my email, and checked my text messages. Flipping back to Uber to see how soon my driver would arrive, a dialogue box popped up asking for my name, address, and phone number. "I guess I need to re-authenticate my credentials," I thought to myself and proceeded to provide the information. Then another dialogue box asked for my employment history, annual salary, and Social Security number.

"What the $#%&," I exclaimed. "This is crazy! What kind of insanity is going on at Uber?" Then I realized the insanity was mine. In the midst of doing three or four things at once, I had unwittingly begun to apply for an Uber credit card. Yikes! Exiting out immediately, I discovered I'd walked to the wrong waiting area and had to run to a completely different terminal to catch my ride.

The myth of multitasking, like Big Foot, the Abominable Snowman, and the Loch Ness Monster, is that it actually exists. It does not. It's not possible for the human brain to simultaneously process two activities at the same time. What we call multitasking is not multitasking at all but task switching with a side of neurological tomfoolery. "When we think we are multitasking, our brains are actually moving from one thing to the next, and our performance degrades for each new task we add to the mix. Multitasking gives us a neurological high so we think we are doing better and better, when actually we are doing worse and worse," writes MIT professor Sherry Turkle in *Reclaiming Conversation*.[23]

There's real data on how much performance degrades for each new task we add to the mix. A research study conducted by the American Psychological Association discovered that multitasking decreased a person's ability to complete a job by 40%, almost doubling the amount of time it takes. Additionally, task switchers' IQ drops by fifteen points, comparable to the effects of smoking marijuana.[24] This is how in 2017, the wrong winner was announced for best picture at the Oscars and how 1.6 million automobile accidents occur every year from texting while driving. And this is how I came to apply for a credit card while I was reading my email, checking my text messages, and walking to the shared ride zone at O'Hare airport. What's the answer to this vexing problem? Here are three multitasking solutions.

Solution One: Focus

The first solution to multitasking is uni-tasking. Uni-tasking is disciplining yourself to do one thing at a time and one thing only. The reason why this requires discipline is that the brain rewards task switching with a hit of dopamine. This chemical high feels good, but, like any drug, its false sense of euphoria fails us. Doing only one thing at a time means turning off your phone, disabling your notifications, and focusing like a laser on the task, or the person, before you. It's being fully present in the moment and being completely aware of the needs of the moment.

Let me warn you, however, your first attempts at this will fail. You'll find yourself grabbing for a WMD—wireless mobile device—for a dopamine hit within a matter of minutes. But I assure you, after a few weeks that addiction will wear off, and you'll be able think again in a focused, concentrated manner. And that's a competitive advantage. Who spends time thinking anymore? With everyone in business running around like chickens with their head cut off, a leader who can think, think deeply, and think strategically will win. Make sure that leader is you.

Solution Two: Batch

What do you do, then, with all that email and all those text messages? You can't just let them go. Can you? Maybe some of them you can (See Solution Three: Prune), but most of them have to be attended to. Batching is how you do that.

We tell our salespeople that when they have to make a bunch of outbound calls to carve out a block of time and do them all at once, rather than making one or two calls every hour or so. A protected time block allows salespeople to do this work without interruption, and grouping calls together gets them into a rhythm that generates momentum. That's batching: completing common tasks together during an allotted period of time in a way that accelerates their execution. And, just like you would with your salespeople, make a game out of how many emails and text messages you can process in any given batch.

Instead of a constant stream of digital interruptions, I have three batching sessions in my day where I process my texts and email. At first, these time blocks went on forever, but now I execute in them quickly and efficiently. As a result, I have a freedom and a joy in my day that's absolutely priceless.

Solution 3: Prune

"I have yet to see an executive, regardless of rank or station, who could not consign something like a quarter of the demands on his time to the wastepaper basket without anybody noticing their disappearance," Peter Drucker again advises us in *The Effective Executive*.[25] It's still true today (except for the wastepaper basket thing). The question, of course, is which 25%? That's why I've used the imagery of pruning for this third multitasking solution.

Why do grape growers prune their vines? So the vines produce more fruit. It's just as simple as that. Instead of having the energy of the plant being used for big beautiful leaves and long flowing branches, they want the energy of the plant being used for growing grapes. That's how they make their living. The workplace parallel is perfect. Your energy can be diverted in a typical day to dozens of things that deliver no real business outcome—big beautiful leaves and long flowing branches—a total waste of a time. Ask yourself, what activities contribute directly to achieving your goals? What are the most important things of the most important things? What are your highest priorities? Define these. Do these. Obsess over these and let everything else go.

Multitasking, then, becomes unnecessary because you'll only be doing that which is essential: producing fruit. Whether you've applied for a credit card while reading your email, checking your text messages, and rushing to catch an Uber, or done something even more costly multitasking, stop it. It will ultimately derail your leadership career. Start becoming a uni-tasker—doing one thing at a time and one thing only— batching your digital communication and getting rid of the things you shouldn't be doing at all.

Derailer Three: Working Weekends

A few weeks ago, my wife and I went out to dinner to celebrate our anniversary. When we got to one of our favorite restaurants, all the tables were full, and we ended up sitting on two quiet stools at the end of the bar. We had the most wonderful evening, and our waitress surprised us with a free anniversary dessert. Yeah!

Halfway through our date, another couple walked in, and as with us, all the tables were full, and they sat at the bar. After ordering their drinks, both the man and the woman pulled out their smartphones, started scrolling through them and continued scrolling the entire evening. When our surprise dessert arrived, the husband, looking up from his phone, asked us how many years we had been married, and we ended up talking with him for a bit. They, too, he told us, were on a date night. Her parents had come down to watch their kids and they decided to go out to eat. So how were they spending their time? Catching up with work on their phones! There's so much wrong with this situation on so many levels, but I wanted to scream at them, "Stop working on the weekend!"

Why Do We Work on the Weekend?

Why do we work on the weekend? Ironically, it's not because we're hard workers. It's because we don't use our time wisely during the week. We take hours to answer email rather than being crisp and concise. We go to unnecessary meetings, and the meetings that are necessary wander aimlessly. And we take long coffee breaks, longer lunches, and an even longer time checking the news, ESPN, YouTube, Facebook, and Twitter. It's amazing anything gets done! Discipline during the week is the first secret to enjoying the weekend. Discipline in three areas: meetings, email, and media.

1. Meeting Discipline

John Anner has led not one but two wildly successful organizations. The first, a for-profit company he started with only a few hundred bucks, is the Independent Press Association. This start-up grew to a multimillion-dollar enterprise in a very competitive marketplace. The second is a not-for-profit organization, the East Meets West Foundation. The East Meets West Foundation provides clean water, medical treatment, and education to developing countries, primarily in Southeast Asia. "The most useful thing I've ever done in any organization is train the staff on how to have efficient meetings," Anner says in the book *168 Hours: You Have More Time Than You Think* by Laura Vanderkam.[26]

What are his rules for meetings? No one goes to a meeting who doesn't need to be there. Every meeting has an agenda. At the beginning of the meeting, the meeting leader spells out the goals for the meeting; and at the end of the meeting the participants go back through the agenda to review what needs to get done before the next meeting. Meetings in his organization are short, sharply focus affairs that begin on time and end on time. By increasing meeting efficiency, Anner says, "It gives me *at least* ten extra hours a week."

That's the meaning of meeting discipline.

2. Email Discipline

Like meetings, some email doesn't need to be answered at all. Read them and move on. For email that does need answering, make yours short and sweet: six sentences. With the one hundred or so emails we send and receive each day, six sentences is all anyone has the time to read and digest. Batch your email in a morning and afternoon work session, instead of letting it interrupt you all throughout the day and derailing your productivity. After three email exchanges back and forth with someone, stop hitting reply and have a live conversation.

3. Media Discipline

Now turn off all your notifications, disable your browser, and remove YouTube, Instagram, Facebook, Twitter, or whatever from your work computer. Work at work. Ruthlessly eliminate digital distractions from your day. Play in the evening and on the weekend. No, you don't need to be hermit at the office to get all your work done in a week, but you do need to be careful about endless chatter. Conversations over a cup of coffee or lunch together with coworkers is perfectly appropriate. Just don't linger. Be friendly, cordial, and kind. Then get back to business.

What Do You Do on the Weekend?

Discipline during the week gets us to the weekend, but what do we do once we're there? All of us are given sixty hours to invest in ourselves, our families, and our friends every Friday at 6:00 p.m. This block of time extends to Monday morning at 6:00 a.m. With the right habits, these sixty hours can become a powerful, pleasurable presence in your life.

1. Reconnect

Weekends should first be about relationships. Our crazy busy work weeks leave little time to foster deep, heartfelt connection with the ones whom we love the most. Spend time with family and friends. Go on a date with your spouse and play with your children. As a person of faith, I also take extra time on the weekend to connect with God at church and to read the Bible.

2. Rest

Sleep is also one of the casualties of our crazy busy weeks. Late weeknights can cut sleep short, or anxious thoughts can leave us lying awake for hours. Take the weekend to catch up. Go to bed early, sleep in, or both. Take naps and move at a slower pace. Your body will thank you.

3. Recreate

Whatever you do, don't plop yourself in front of the television all weekend long. Get out of the house. Take a hike. Go for a run. Play Frisbee. Walk in the park. Move! Recreation is restorative for the body, mind, and emotions. It's what Alexa Pang describes in his brilliant book *Rest* as "active rest," explaining, "When we think of rest, we usually think of passive activities: taking a nap, lying on the couch, watching sports on television, or binge-watching a popular TV series. That's one form of rest. But physical activity is more restful than we expect, and mental rest more active than we realize."[27]

4. Refresh

Finally, do the things you love, the things that refresh your soul and renew your mind. I love cooking, so I cook big meals on the weekend. I love good beer, so we'll visit a local microbrewery. I love a good book—not a business book—so I read the latest novel at a leisurely pace. I'm also learning how do woodworking and am having a ton of fun making handcrafted projects. What these things do for me is turn off my brain from thinking about work and bring calm and composure to my emotions. I didn't always live this way, weekends used to be as wild as the week, but ultimately, I hit the wall and had to do something different. Dramatically different. Disconnecting at 6:00 p.m. on Fridays, I now walk into a weekend that's full of joy and satisfaction and walk out of it refreshed and energized for the week.

I'm guessing that's pretty much your story too and challenge you to reclaim the sixty hours of freedom that's yours from Friday to Sunday to reconnect, rest, recreate, and refresh. One final note, doing all of these wonderful activities on the weekend means being a bit more strategic during the week about household responsibilities. If you're not careful, you'll exchange one set of work activities for another: paying the bills and mowing the lawn, washing the laundry and cleaning the house. With some preplanning and ingenuity, however, you can get these things done before Saturday and Sunday and have plenty of time for weekend wellness.

Sales Leadership and Self-Leadership

While you're Googling sleep hygiene—something I recommended a few pages ago if you're hitting the snooze button more than once in a morning—Google the term "sinkhole" as well. What you'll find is extraordinary video footage of the ground opening up and swallowing roads, houses, cars, and anything else in its path.

What happens with a sinkhole is ground water below the surface of the earth dries up and structures above the surface collapse into it. It's a crisis affecting states like California and Florida, which have been overrun with commercial development. Get the point? Your outer world is dependent on your inner world to survive. If your inner world dries up, and nothing is done to replenish it, your outer world will collapse.

Here's the ultimate bottom line of this book: Successful sales leadership flows from the springs of successful self-leadership. Your outer world needs your inner world to be healthy and strong. Refusing to be driven by the urgency of manic mornings, the myth of multitasking, and working on the weekend is not just a nice suggestion for having a happier life. It's much, much more than that. It's critical instruction for a long, rich, and rewarding leadership career, untouched by the derailment that so many of your peers will experience. Follow this path without fail, please. Your future self, and those who love you, will thank you for doing so.

And that's the point, isn't it?

SALES LEADERSHIP RESOURCES

Digital versions of these resources are available online at
www.billzipp.com/salessuccess.

Trust Triad Questionnaire

TRUST TRIAD QUESTION	Almost Never / Almost Always				
1. Do you practice what you preach? Are the actions you take as a leader fully aligned with words you say?	1	2	3	4	5
2. Do you honor your word? When you say you're going to do something, do you do it *without exception*?	1	2	3	4	5

3. Are you genuine and real? Have you dropped the chest-thumping bravado and ego-driven games that so many sales leaders play?	1	2	3	4	5
4. Do you say sorry when you're wrong? When you make a mistake, do you admit it—openly and honestly—and move on?	1	2	3	4	5
5. Are you a living example of the mission and values of your company? Are you asking people to do things that you're not doing yourself on a consistent basis?	1	2	3	4	5
6. Do you have a clear grasp of the key responsibilities of your position and fulfill those responsibilities at the highest levels of excellence?	1	2	3	4	5
7. Do you have a reliable system that captures your activities and appointments, so no detail or deadline gets dropped?	1	2	3	4	5
8. Do you process your email in a prompt and productive manner, getting back to team members who contact you during the work week within 24 hours?	1	2	3	4	5

9. Do you facilitate the meetings you run in a businesslike manner, starting on time, ending on time, and staying on track with the items on the agenda?	1	2	3	4	5
10. Is your physical appearance and dress sharp and professional, always appropriate for the various business situations in which you find yourself?	1	2	3	4	5
11. Are you fully present in the meetings you attend? Have you eliminated all distractions (and potential distractions), like a ringing phone or pinging notifications?	1	2	3	4	5
12. Do you actively listen to the people you're with in a meeting? Do you pay attention to what they're really saying, not just their words but the emotions behind them?	1	2	3	4	5
13. Does your physical posture reflect your personal presence? Do you lean forward, make eye contact, nod your head, fully engaged in the conversation?	1	2	3	4	5

14. Do you ask good questions? Do you help people clarify their thoughts by posing open-ended queries that allow them to explore the issues at hand more deeply?	1	2	3	4	5
15. Do you make a point to find something you can honestly affirm, compliment, or praise in the course of your conversations?	1	2	3	4	5
16. Are you fully prepared for your team meetings, so your mind and emotions are confident and calm? This includes preparations related to physical arrangements and technology.	1	2	3	4	5
17. Do you schedule extra time before and/or after your team meetings to make informal connections with the people in attendance?	1	2	3	4	5
18. Have you thought through ways to make your team meetings fully interactive, so you aren't the only one talking in them?	1	2	3	4	5

19. Do you have a way to remind yourself to stop, take a deep breath, make eye contact, and smile at the beginning, middle, and end of your team meetings?	1	2	3	4	5
20. Do you make a point to authentically thank, recognize, or praise someone in attendance and/ or the entire group at your team meetings?	1	2	3	4	5
TOTAL			out of 100		

The Motivation Matrix

PURPOSE: Primary	PURPOSE: Secondary
What is this person's primary purpose in sales? Fortune, fame, freedom, or family?	What is this person's secondary purpose in sales? Fortune, fame, freedom, or family?
VISION: Long Term	**VISION: Short Term**
What is a big tangible dream this person wants to achieve?	What will move this person closer to achieving that dream every quarter, every month, every week, every day?

Salesperson's Name	Date	Biggest Motivational Insight
1		
2		
3		
4		
5		
6		
7		
8		

Weekly Affirmation Worksheet

WEEK ONE DATE:					
Salesperson's Name	M	T	W	T	F
	☐	☐	☐	☐	☐
	☐	☐	☐	☐	☐
	☐	☐	☐	☐	☐
	☐	☐	☐	☐	☐
	☐	☐	☐	☐	☐
	☐	☐	☐	☐	☐
	☐	☐	☐	☐	☐
	☐	☐	☐	☐	☐
WEEK TWO DATE:					
Salesperson's Name	M	T	W	T	F
	☐	☐	☐	☐	☐
	☐	☐	☐	☐	☐
	☐	☐	☐	☐	☐
	☐	☐	☐	☐	☐
	☐	☐	☐	☐	☐
	☐	☐	☐	☐	☐
	☐	☐	☐	☐	☐

	☐	☐	☐	☐	☐
WEEK THREE DATE:					
Salesperson's Name	M	T	W	T	F
	☐	☐	☐	☐	☐
	☐	☐	☐	☐	☐
	☐	☐	☐	☐	☐
	☐	☐	☐	☐	☐
	☐	☐	☐	☐	☐
	☐	☐	☐	☐	☐
	☐	☐	☐	☐	☐
	☐	☐	☐	☐	☐
WEEK FOUR DATE:					
Salesperson's Name	M	T	W	T	F
	☐	☐	☐	☐	☐
	☐	☐	☐	☐	☐
	☐	☐	☐	☐	☐
	☐	☐	☐	☐	☐
	☐	☐	☐	☐	☐
	☐	☐	☐	☐	☐
	☐	☐	☐	☐	☐
	☐	☐	☐	☐	☐

Sales Goal Grid

Salesperson:	
Sales Performance Goal	
Sales Process Goals Specific, repeated activities that move a person closer to achieving a sales performance goal	1.
	2.
	3.
	4.

Sales Coaching Assessment Worksheet

Salesperson:		
Sales Performance Goal		
Sales Process Goals Specific, repeated activities that move a person closer to achieving a sales performance goal	1.	
	Competence ☐ Low to Some ☐ Mostly High	Commitment ☐ Low to Variable ☐ Mostly High
	Circle Development Level: 1 2 3 4	
	2.	
	Competence ☐ Low to Some ☐ Mostly High	Commitment ☐ Low to Variable ☐ Mostly High
	Circle Development Level: 1 2 3 4	

	3.
	Competence ☐ Low to Some ☐ Mostly High | **Commitment** ☐ Low to Variable ☐ Mostly High
	Circle Development Level: 1 2 3 4
	4.
	Competence ☐ Low to Some ☐ Mostly High | **Commitment** ☐ Low to Variable ☐ Mostly High
	Circle Development Level: 1 2 3 4

Sales Coaching Style Strategies

Salesperson:	
Development Level for Process Goal One:	
Sales coaching strategies for Process Goal One	
Development Level for Process Goal Two:	
Sales coaching strategiess for Process Goal Two	
Development Level for Process Goal Three:	
Sales coaching strategiesfor Process Goal Three	
Development Level for Process Goal Four:	
Sales coaching strategies for Process Goal Four	

Team Meeting Preparation Template

Inspiration

- Who's achieved something significant in the last few weeks? New appointments set? New logos won? New skills acquired? New deals done? How can you acknowledge this in a meaningful way at an upcoming meeting?
- Who's reached a significant milestone in the last few weeks? Consecutive months over goal? An extraordinarily large deal? The completion of a special project? How can you acknowledge this in a meaningful way at an upcoming meeting?
- Who's had something positive happen in their personal life in the last few weeks? A birthday, an anniversary, the birth of a baby, a new house, a new car, a graduation? How can you celebrate this together as a team?

Instruction

- What's a critical sales skill that most everyone needs refreshed on? What article, video, case study, or role-play can you use to sharpen your team's ability related to this skill?
- What's a new sales skill your team needs to master due to a shift in the marketplace? What article, video, case study, or role-play can you use to sharpen everyone's ability related to this skill?
- What non-sales skill, like time management, cross-functional communication, or financial acumen, does your team need to master? What content will you use to help develop these skills in their life?
- Interaction
- What two-way communication strategies can you employ in providing the instruction above? Discussion groups? Learning exercises? Town hall open forums?

- What difficult but important questions about what's going on in the marketplace need to be discussed openly and honestly as a team? The quality of your product and/or service? The terms for your product and/or service? A new competitor? The economy?
- Who other than you—both inside and outside your team—can be deputized to help provide inspiration, instruction, interaction, and information in your meetings? What senior leaders can you invite to your meetings so the members of your team begin to build executive sponsorship within the organization?

Information

- Where is individual and team progress toward goal for the current month, quarter, and year?
- What new product, product development, and/or pricing details need to be communicated to the team?
- What upcoming dates on the company's calendar need to be kept top of mind?
- What helpful personnel policies need to be reviewed?

Historical Interviewing Preparation Worksheet

Sales Skill One:

Interviewing Questions:

Sales Skill Two:

Interviewing Questions:

Sales Skill Three:

Interviewing Questions:

Sales Skill Four:

Interviewing Questions:

Sales Skill Five:

Interviewing Questions:

Salesperson or Sales Manager?

Column A	Rating							Column B
You love to sell.	3	2	1	0	1	2	3	You love to lead.
You love the sales process.	3	2	1	0	1	2	3	You love people.
You love the spotlight.	3	2	1	0	1	2	3	You can work on the sidelines.
Cross-functional communication exhausts you.	3	2	1	0	1	2	3	You communicate well cross-functionally.
You work hard to leave early on Friday afternoon.	3	2	1	0	1	2	3	You like to work on the weekend.
TOTAL: *Numbers to the left of 0*								**TOTAL:** *Numbers to the right of 0*
Subtract Column A's Total from Column B's Total								**OVERALL TOTAL:**

Digital versions of these resources are available online at www.billzipp.com/salessuccess.

ABOUT THE AUTHOR

 Bill Zipp helps busy CEOs, heads of sales, and frontline managers become better leaders, grow their people, and hit their number.

Bill has over twenty years of experience with high-growth companies and agile startups, as well as established businesses stuck on sales plateaus. He's worked with hundreds of sales leaders around the world, from ADP to Avalara, Businessolver to SAP Concur. Many of these companies experienced dramatic revenue growth while working with him, some doubling and tripling annual sales. For more information, check out www.billzipp.com.

Bill lives in Corvallis, Oregon, home of Oregon State University and the beloved orange and black of the Oregon State Beavers. He's married to Denise and has three amazing adult children—Beckie, Ricky, and Renee.

ENDNOTES

1   Bill George, *Authentic Leadership* (San Francisco, CA: Jossey Bass, 2003) 65.

2   Richard Boyatzis and Annie McKee, *Resonant Leadership* (Boston, MA: HBS Press, 2005) 120.

3   Viktor Frankl, *Man's Search for Meaning* (Boston, MA: Beacon Press, 1946) 10.

4   Rodd Wagner and James K. Harter, *12: The Elements of Great Managing* (New York, NY: Gallup Press, 2006) 52.

5   Tom Rath and Donald O. Clifton, *How Full Is Your Bucket?* (New York, NY: Gallup Press, 2004) 55-57.

6   John Mackey and Raj Sisodia, *Conscious Capitalism* (Boston, MA: HBS Press, 2013) 217.

7   Angela Duckworth, *Grit: The Power of Passion and Perseverance* (New York, NY: Scribner, 2016) 269.

8   Daniel Goleman, Richard Boyatzis, and Annie McKee, *Primal Leadership* (Boston, MA: HBS Press, 2002) 5, 6.

9   Kim Scott, *Radical Candor* (New York, NY: St. Martin's Press, 2017) xii.

10   Larry Bossidy and Ram Charan, *Execution: The Discipline of Getting Things Done* (New York, NY: Crown Business, 2002) 74.

11   James Clear, *Atomic Habits* (New York, NY: Avery, 2018) 16.

12   Paul Hersey and Ken Blanchard, *Management of Organizational Behavior* (New York, NY: Prentice Hall, 1982).

13   John Doerr, *Measure What Matters* (New York, NY: Portfolio/ Penguin, 2018) 36.

14   Stephen R. Covey, *The 7 Habits of Highly Effective People* (New York, NY: Simon and Schuster, 1989) 237.

15   Jim Collins, *Good to Great* (New York, NY: Harper Business, 2001) 54.

16   Geoff Smart and Randy Street, *Who: The A Method of Hiring* (New York: NY: Ballantine Books, 2008) 70.

17   Bradford D. Smart, *Topgrading* (New York, NY: Portfolio/Penguin, 2005) xix.

18   Smart, *Topgrading*, 310-312.

19   Smart and Street, *Who: The A Method of Hiring,* 107.

20   Benson Smith and Tony Rutigliano, *Discover Your Sales Strengths* (New York, NY: Warner Business Books, 2003) 158.

21   Laura Vanderkam, *What the Most Successful People Do Before Breakfast* (New York, NY: Portfolio/Penguin, 2012) Kindle edition, 189.

22   Peter F. Drucker, *The Effective Executive* (New York, NY: Harper Business, 1966) 112.

23   Sherry Turkle, *Reclaiming Conversation* (New York, NY: Penguin Press, 2015) 213.

24 Daniel J. Levitin, *The Organized Mind* (New York, NY: Dutton, 2014) 96.

25 Drucker, *The Effective Executive*, 37.

26 Laura Vanderkam, *168 Hours: You Have More Time Than You Think* (New York, NY: Portfolio/Penguin, 2010) 81, 82.

27 Alex Soojung-Kim Pang, *Rest* (New York, NY: Basic Books, 2016) 12.